MUSINGS

Social, Political and Religious Criticism

by

William Charles Arbaugh

Erbach Books
Trafford Publishing

© Copyright 2004 William Charles Arbaugh.
All rights reserved. No part of this publication may be reproduced, stored in a retrieval system, or transmitted, in any form or by any means, electronic, mechanical, photocopying, recording, or otherwise, without the written prior permission of the author.

Note for Librarians: a cataloguing record for this book that includes Dewey Decimal Classification and US Library of Congress numbers is available from the Library and Archives of Canada. The complete cataloguing record can be obtained from their online database at:
www.collectionscanada.ca/amicus/index-e.html
ISBN 1-4120-4280-1
Printed in Victoria, BC, Canada

TRAFFORD

Offices in Canada, USA, Ireland, UK and Spain
This book was published on-demand in cooperation with Trafford Publishing. On-demand publishing is a unique process and service of making a book available for retail sale to the public taking advantage of on-demand manufacturing and Internet marketing. On-demand publishing includes promotions, retail sales, manufacturing, order fulfilment, accounting and collecting royalties on behalf of the author.
Book sales for North America and international:
Trafford Publishing, 6E–2333 Government St.,
Victoria, BC v8T 4P4 CANADA
phone 250 383 6864 (toll-free 1 888 232 4444)
fax 250 383 6804; email to orders@trafford.com
Book sales in Europe:
Trafford Publishing (UK) Ltd., Enterprise House, Wistaston Road Business Centre,
Wistaston Road, Crewe, Cheshire CW2 7RP UNITED KINGDOM
phone 01270 251 396 (local rate 0845 230 9601)
facsimile 01270 254 983; orders.uk@trafford.com
Order online at:
www.trafford.com/robots/04-2087.html

10 9 8 7 6 5 4 3 2

Dedicated to

St. James Lutheran Church

Portland, Oregon

Preface

It is often said that in polite conversation the topics of religion and politics should be avoided but how long can most of us carry an engaging conversation on the weather? Religion and politics are vital subjects reflecting the basics in love of God and love of neighbor. The 39 essays here presented express the desire to relate the Christian faith to the world in which we live.

Years ago my custom of writing paragraphs of opinion in frequent letters to family and friends expanded into pages of commentary on topics of personal interest, generally reflecting my current reading. One of the recipients of these writings was my friend Joe Smith, pastor of St. James Lutheran Church in Portland, Oregon, and after I became related to that congregation he invited me to write such a page of opinion for occasional distribution through the congregation's newsletter. This was the beginning of "Musings" which grew to become the source of most (not all) of the essays in this book.

Referring to the twin topics of religion and politics, it should be said that I write from the perspective of Lutheran theology, conscious of the four marks of the church, as stated in the Creed: the "one holy catholic and apostolic church". In this context I consider important the descriptive words "evangelical," referring to the gospel (not the current popular usage) and "catholic," referring broadly to Christendom.

As noted in Chapter 31, "the witness of this church in society flows from its identity as a community that lives from and for the gospel". Moreover, "as a prophetic presence, this church has the obligation…to identify the power of sin present in social structures," thus necessarily examining the political structures of our society.

There are Christian groups today who call for moral absolutes within rigid lines of authority from a Bible interpreted as regulatory or legislative. The Lutheran understanding, however, holds the Bible as the record of God's saving grace and in the cradle of the written Word there is the Incarnate Word, to quote a famous Christmas sermon by Martin Luther. With his advice we should worship the Child and not the cradle.

The need to guard against inflexible and authoritarian patterns should be clear in hearing an old Scottish prayer, "Lord, grant that we are always completely in the right for we shall surely never change our minds," as quoted in Chapter 4. Without rigid absolutes, the community of faith or the congregation has an important role in showing that "faith is active in love".

Much appreciated is the encouragement I have received from numerous readers. Some have repeatedly suggested a wider distribution of these "Musings," including Earl Sakrison, Eugene Kindschuh and various members of St. James Church.

Also appreciated is the assistance given me in overcoming frustrating problems with the computer, especially, my neighbor James Baxendale and my son and daughter-in-law Stephen and Elizabeth—Stephen for taming the computer and Elizabeth for making the manuscript acceptable to the publisher. She especially deserves a hearty accolade.

William C. Arbaugh

June 24, 2004
The Nativity of
St. John the Baptist

CONTENTS

1	Don't Cut Off the Roots	1
2	The Unholy Holy Land	4
3	"God Bless Us—Everyone"	7
4	Law as a Schoolmaster	10
5	Who is Guilty? Who Decides?	13
6	Think Globally, Act Globally	16
7	Structures for World Community	19
8	Understanding 1492 and 1969	22
9	Our Brother's Keeper	25
10	Labels: Liberal and Conservative	28
11	Classrooms Without Festivals	31
12	Lutherans in London	34
13	Worship and the Arts	37
14	Episcopalians and Lutherans	40
15	Elian and the Miami Cubans	44
16	Postage Stamps Reflect Society	48
17	Florence Nightingale and Clara Maass	51
18	Christians: In Community or Loners	54
19	Palestinian Land	57
20	A Christmas Carol	60
21	Quo Vadis?	63
22	Lessons from Another Colossus	66
23	Privatization and Globalization	69
24	The Public Square and the Church	73
25	Healing in Retribution?	77
26	A Focus on Pain and Reaction	80
27	Government No Longer the Enemy	84
28	Views from New Zealand	88
29	Authoritarianism and the War on Terror	92
30	Bonhoeffer's Warning of Fascism	95

31	Between Vision and Reality	98
32	An International Church	101
33	The Trials of Democracy	105
34	Foreboding in Issues Foreign and Domestic	109
35	War and Consequences	116
	Roger Williams	120
36	A Century of Flight	123
	An Unthinkable Thought	126
	Sensitive to the Anguished Debate	127
37	Political Rallies Sharpen the Message	130
38	New Forms of Christianity	137
	A 21st-Century Feudalism	141
39	Piety and Fascism	144
40	Church and State: Dialogue or Clash	150

1

Don't Cut Off the Roots

November 7, 1998

The frequently told stories at family gatherings may be boring to some but they serve a purpose in building family identification. Imagine the difficulty, the virtual impossibility, of having a personal identity without some roots. An understanding of one's heritage is important, for a person, a family, a nation or a faith. One may move away from the identity of the family but the early influence remains. Attending a conference at First Congregational Church in Portland (Nov. 7), I heard an engaging presentation on the Hispanic presence in the history of Oregon.

An intriguing thought is the problem of the very word "Hispanic," which is being used with increasing frequency. The speaker, a professor from the University of Washington, Dr. Erasmo Gamboa, noted that this is becoming a favored term in the merchandising programs of major corporations as they recognize the buying power of this group. He recommended appreciative use of the term "Hispanic" but he also pointed to unhappy associations in that the word cuts off some roots of heritage. Instead of being a Cuban-American, a Mexican-American, or a Peruvian-American one becomes simply Hispanic. In parallel terms, one might combine Irish-Americans, Italian-Americans, German-Americans and Polish-Americans in one grand term: European-Americans. The effect, however, is that it minimizes one's heritage. Nevertheless, the speaker said that the term "Hispanic" can be useful. In a publication on Hispanics in Oregon a page is devoted to "What some people choose to call themselves," and there are diverse opinions:

- "I perceive myself as Afro-Cuban-American. I find I am obligated all the time to identify myself as Hispanic... My children are great—they think they are Cubans. Both grew up in Portland." —Armando Laguardia (Cuba)
- "I'm obviously a Mexican American. I was born in Medford." —Roberto Gozalez (United States)

- "The first time I heard the term Hispanic was when I came to the States and had to fill out forms. I just fill them out differently each time —Indian, Black, Hispanic —who do I identify with? I am all of them." —Luciano Praño (Peru)[1]

Arrest Lewis and Clark?

In his lecture Dr. Gamboa offered some insightful thoughts. Stating that Hispanics were in the Oregon Territory before the formation of a national identity in 1776, the audience then chuckled when he mentioned that when Spain heard about the Lewis and Clark expedition, they sent a detachment to arrest Lewis and Clark as "illegals". Hispanics, he said, were the first non-native people in this territory and they were a significant factor in the development of the Pacific Northwest. "Nearly four centuries ago Spanish explorers sailed along the Pacific Coast and recorded detailed observations about the land and its inhabitants.[2]

Moreover, Hispanics made significant contributions. In the mid 1800s Mexican mules were bred and trained for use in pack trains, some pack trains said to number 1500 mules. This was the transportation system. In cattle ranching and cattle drives the vaqueros were the original cowboys, traveling north from the Southwest (for example, "chaps" is from the Spanish chaparreras). Labor on the railroads, especially during World War II employed many Hispanics—up to 80% Mexican on the Southern Pacific in the 1940s.

Are maps truthful?

Much as we wish to be balanced and unprejudiced, it is hard to avoid influences from unexpected sources. Why should we suspect maps of arrogantly hiding the truth? When I was a child the world map on my bedroom wall was the one familiar to many of us with the vertical and horizontal lines all evenly spaced. This was the grid named after the Flemish geographer Mercator in the 16th century. Europe was at the center, befitting the age, but why was Scandinavia larger than the sub-continent of India? Why was Greenland so large and Africa small? One answer, is that the meridian lines did not converge at the poles. However, a second answer is that the scale was reduced for everything south of Europe and the United States,

---

[1] Erasmo Gamboa and Carolyn Buam (eds.), *Nosotros : The Hispanic People of Oregon* (Oregon Council for the Humanities, Portland, Or.), p. 5.

[2] Gamboa, *Nosotros*, p. 21.

implying that everything south is not important. Thus Alaska appears larger than Mexico, whereas the opposite is true.

What's the actual distance, say from San Diego to the south of Mexico? I had occasion a few weeks ago to look this up because our son James was about to make this trip in a helicopter. Because of the natural disasters in Central America, Mexican authorities contracted with a California company for two additional helicopters for relief missions. This company needed an extra pilot and James was available so with two hours' notice he was on his way. He and another pilot were to fly two Hueys from Bakersfield to San Diego, cross the border at Tijuana and then down to the southern state of Chiapas. It doesn't look far on the map but the distance from Tijuana to Chiapas is actually close to 2,500 miles, whereas Blaine (Wa.) to San Diego—top to bottom—is about 1,500 miles.[3] The Mexican flight was equivalent to flying from Seattle to San Diego and then back up to Portland and in a Huey it took five days. James reported that there were villages which were completely isolated and there were people in desperate need. The destruction in some areas was horrendous. And this was before hurricane Mitch.

Whether it's because of maps or other influences we need to guard against any form of arrogance or superiority. The lecturer, Dr. Gamboa, did not say much about discrimination, although he mentioned a letter he discovered which had been written by a Mexican who had been jailed in Walla Walla during World War 2. He was in jail on two counts: (a) he was illegal and (b) he was a draft dodger!

As with a name, so also with heritage. Respect and understanding are needed. In Gamboa's words, "Esta complejidad hace la pregunta 'cómo llamarnos' dificil de contestar. Latino, chicano, mexicano americano, sudamericano, e hispano—... las posibilidades son innumerables." Conclusion: Pero todos requieren respeto y entendimiento.

---

[3] Text books now have maps with a more accurate portrayal of proportions and distances than those with the Mercator projections. Our church's Division for Global Mission has made use of a map in which given areas are depicted in proportion to actual size, as developed in the 1970s by a German cartographer, Peters.

2

The Unholy Holy Land

December 12, 1998

With the approach of Christmas we think of Bethlehem and many of us have the desire to visit that key point in what we have known as the Holy Land. In fact, President Clinton's official schedule this month will include some time for a "personal visit" to Bethlehem. A century ago the author of "O Little Town of Bethlehem," Phllips Brooks, was inspired to write the carol when he sat on a hillside overlooking the town one quiet night. But all is not quiet and peaceful or "still" at this time. The editor of *The Lutheran*, Edgar Trexler, wrote in the current issue that "The unholy land itself is a paradox of the Prince of Peace's birth-place and a territory over which people have fought bitterly."

"Paradox" is the pivotal word, considered in several facets. For one thing, that land is holy in the terms of three great religions: Judaism, Islam and Christianity. It is noteworthy that all three faiths are monotheistic. Against the image of Islam's aggressive early growth with the power of the sword, it should be remembered that Muslims then considered Jews and Christians "brothers of the Book". Abraham is a patriarch to Christian, Jew and Muslim. How is it then that there should be such enmity among those whose faith has tied them to a holy land?

Moreover, there is a cloud of prejudice and discrimination in popular images. Recall the accusations against Arabs after the Oklahoma City bombing. There is also the need to distinguish anti-Semitism from anti-Zionism. There can be no defense for anti-Semitism, which is plain and simple prejudicial discrimination. But Zionism is a debatable opin-ion on justification of a political state of Israel. The question, in other words, concerns justifying the establishment (in 1948) of the state of Israel. Aside from the current reality, many claims have been made to the Holy Land but there is no common yardstick of measurement and each claim has a counter-claim.

The Unholy Holy Land

Consider first the biblical basis to Israel's claim to Palestine, the land which God promised to Abraham and to his descendants, noted in Genesis 12 and 15. The problem is not its validity to the Jew, but interpretations which are different to others. Christians and Muslims also trace lines of faith from Father Abraham. Muslims continue to claim God's blessing on Ishamel in Genesis 17 and Christians interpret the Old Testament in the perspective of the New Testament, the new covenant.

In the second place there have been numerous political claims. Zionism was a dream for many Jews who faced bitter persecution under anti-Semitic legislation in Eastern Europe in the late 1800s. The savage German persecution of Jews made the world sensitive to Jewish sufferings. Moreover, with the beginning of the Cold War in the late 1940s the United States was not unaware of the benefits of a friendly state (a beachhead) in the Middle East. So it was that with U.S. support the United Nations approved a committee resolution favoring the partition of Palestine. It was not a clear-cut decision and conditions were still debated when independence was proclaimed by the new state of Israel on May 14, 1948.

One of the unresolved problems was that of self-determination. In 1914 the Jews in Palestine numbered 6 or 7% of the population, changing to 650,000 or 33% of the population by 1946, two years before independence. The continued influx of Jewish refugees meant changing demographics, causing problems for regional self-determination. A major fault of Zionism has been its refusal to recognize the existence of Palestinian Arab refugees who had been displaced without any compensation.

A third argument by which Israel has claimed the land of Palestine is historical. Although the claim goes back to the time of Abraham, actual control of the land was held by surrounding nations. One study notes that Jews had control of the land for only 414 of nearly 1900 years, the remaining held by Egypt, the Roman Empire, Arabs and Turkey. [1] Whether biblical, political or historical, there is no basis for the Zionist cause acceptable to all. Each claim has a counter-claim.

This year of 1998 marks two fiftieth anniversaries. One is the creation of the state of Israel. Early this year it was observed with considerable attention in the press and broadcast media. Later in the year Portland's Central Library arranged an exhibit which, decidedly

---
[1] Ilene Beatty, *Arab and Jew in the Land of Canaan*. See also Don Peretz, *The Middle East*.

low key, described the plight of the Palestinian people. Quoting from a poster at the exhibit:

> In the wake of the 1948 war that created the state of Israel, more than 750,000 Palestinian refugees were forced into exile... By the end of the war, 418 villages, nearly half of the total number of Palestinian villages existing at the time, had been depopulated and systematically destroyed, their houses blown up or bull-dozed...to ensure that their Christian and Muslim Palestinian owners could not return and live in them again... Moreover, the assets of the Palestinian refugees—their homes, schools, hospitals, churches, mosques, banks...all passed into the possession of the citizens of the nascent Israeli state. Also confiscated...were the refugees' personal assets—their furniture, carpets...and heir-looms—all the accouterments of middle-class life of the Palestinian owners... The total number of refugees of the war constituted 54 percent of the total Palestinian population. Today, half of the 6.4 million Palestinians living around the world are stateless or have only limited citizenship rights.

The other fiftieth anniversary is that of the Universal Declaration of Human Rights. Recently I received a letter signed by three former bishops of our ELCA, including Bishop Herbert Chilstrom, drawing attention to the injustices evident in the Middle East, particularly suffering by the Palestinians. The three bishops have joined other religious leaders (Jewish, Christian and Muslim) in a "Search for Justice and Equality in Palestine/Israel." Praying for the implementation of the Human Rights Declaration, they

- Believe Palestinian-Israeli peace is only possible if based on justice, human rights, and self-determination for Israeli Jews and Palestinian Christians and Muslims.
- Oppose violence against civilians, whether by Palestinians, Jewish settlers, or the Israeli state.
- Want our government to support the rights of Palestinians as well as of Israelis and
- Condemn human rights violations by Israel and the Palestinian Authority.

Singing the carol, "O little town of Bethlehem," we can earnestly desire for all of us the effect of this line: "So God imparts to human hearts The blessings of his heav'n".

3

"God Bless Us—Everyone"

January 20, 1999

At the Performing Arts Center over Christmas there was a delightful presentation of Charles Dickens' "A Christmas Carol" with a stage setting so pleasing that it may be retained for future use. Offering background information, a page in the program booklet noted that

> Dickens lit on the idea for a Christmas story as a statement for social justice after visiting one of London's so-called "ragged schools," one of many organizations instituted to teach the children of the poor: [Dickens wrote] "I have seldom seen, in all the strange and dreadful things I have seen in London and elsewhere, anything so shocking as the dire neglect of soul and body exhibited in these children.

Why does "A Christmas Carol" exert such a powerful tug on the heart? Surely one reason is the highlighting of warm concern for the less fortunate in our life together against the selfishness of a Scrooge who thought only of himself.

Is this concern for others—social concern—linked to our faith? In the liturgy printed in the *Lutheran Book of Worship* there are three post-communion prayers. The first of these appeared in Martin Luther's German Mass, substantially as we have it in English. After giving thanks for the gift of life, the prayer is that God would strengthen us "through this gift, in faith toward you and in fervent love toward one another." Notice the two points: (a) faith toward God and (b) love toward one another. This brings to mind our Lord's instruction on the Great Commandment (love God and love neighbor):

> You shall love the Lord your God with all your heart, and with all your soul, and with all your mind. This is the great and first commandment. And a second is like it, You shall love your neighbor as yourself [Mt. 22:37-38].

Frequently in the use of this post-communion prayer my mind links faith and world by turning to contemporary issues of debate, such as education, medical practice, taxes, and the growing gap between the "haves" and "have nots". It should be noted that in the 1900s children—boys as young as seven—were working in the coal mines 12 hours a day (small bodies could work in the crevices) and it was as recently as the 1920s that industry accepted the standard work day of 8 hours—to the consternation of business, which predicted the ruination of the country.

In the context of the "ragged schools," of Dickens' day, the Sunday School was developed primarily for the teaching of reading and writing to children who were free only on Sundays because they had to work six days a week—in textile mills, in mines, as apprentices, etc. Although churches originally sponsored Sunday Schools, after provision was made for the education of children through governmental means the churches then adapted the idea of the Sunday School primarily for the teaching of religion.

How can we explain the efforts to dismantle our public system of education? If these are good economic times with an impressive stock market and low unemployment and a surplus in state and federal budgets, why is it that we are unwilling to support education and we resort to the lottery (a regressive tax) to educate our children? If we encourage private schools for those who can afford it and siphon off the children with privileged opportunity, we'll drive another wedge in the social division which is now growing.

Consider medical care. It is apparent that the United States offers the best medical care in the world—for those who can pay for it. But here in this country there are some 35 million Americans without medical insurance and the ones who suffer most are children. It often appears that those who make the decisions and those who really profit from this system are the insurance companies.

Recall the words of President Kennedy—ask not what the country can do for you but what you can do for your country. What a contrast to the current self-centered attitudes of me-first-ism! Very few people enjoy paying taxes, but the political mantra to cut taxes has resulted in reforms that are vastly helpful to the wealthy, in some cases reduced the responsibility of business and helped the middle class very little. News reports have indicated that in the two decades of the 1980s and the 1990s the middle class has been diminished and the gap between the haves and the have-nots has been increasing.

"God Bless Us—Everyone"   9

By way of illustration there is an example from Britain. It has been reported that from 1979-1994, highlighted by Margaret Thatcher, "the wealthiest 10 percent of Britons enjoyed a 60 percent increase in net income...and the poorest 10 percent were 1 percent better off."[1] Considering tax reforms which benefit the wealthy, the exclusion of millions of Americans from medical insurance, and the continued assaults on public education, one can imagine a progression of such trends which would result in the growth of a sub-stratum, an under-class in society. Another example from Britain is in the words of Tony Blair, who spoke of his party's vision

> of a Britain that is not just a collection of individuals but a society where a decent community backs up the efforts of individuals within it. That change can't come through market forces. It needs active government, local and national. I start from the simple belief that people are not separate economic actors competing in the marketplace of life. They are citizens of a community. We are social beings, nurtured in families and communities... [2]

The alternative to this view is an individualism which has no concern for others, especially children (who do not have political clout). It would be the triumph of "I've got mine"—and what they've got becomes increasingly meager. Rather than a stark individualism, I'm drawn to Luther's post-communion prayer:

> We give you thanks, almighty God, that you have refreshed us through the healing power of this gift of life; and we pray that in your mercy you would strengthen us, through this gift, **in faith toward you and in fervent love toward one another;** for the sake of Jesus Christ our Lord.

And in the words of Tiny Tim, "God bless us—everyone."

---

[1] Reported by Associated Press, quoting the Institute of Fiscal Studies, *The Oregonian*, May 2, 1997.

[2] Anne Applebaum, "Tony Blair and the New Left," *Foreign Affairs*, March April 1997, p. 48.

4

Law as a Schoolmaster

March 6, 1999

It was said by those who obsessively favored the impeachment of President Clinton that he could not be trusted because he broke the law. It took such a personage as Larry Flynt to note the hypocrisy of those who sat in judgment.

Which law was the president accused of breaking? Was it a matter of not telling the truth or obstructing Ken Starr's pursuit? Judging from accounts of salacious reports at congressional hearings and the popularity of Monica's recent interview, eloquent references to law and justice have often had a hollow sound.

Although the religious right wing frequently speaks of biblical laws and rigid enforcement of laws according to their interpretations, there are problems with simplistic and inflexible solutions. Consider, for example, the defiant opposition to abortion (even granting personhood to the fetus) on the basis of the commandment "You shall not kill". If this is an absolute (no exceptions), then why is there such willingness, often by the same people, to favor capital punishment? Moreover, there's a positive as well as a negative aspect to the commandment, as noted in Martin Luther's Catechism:

> What does this mean for us? We are to fear and love God so that we do not hurt our neighbor in any way but help him in all his physical needs.

It is apparent that the vehement protesters of abortion are not so vehement in enacting social legislation to assist the neighbor in all physical needs. Reading Luther's understanding of the Fifth Commandment, we should ask if we—all of us—are not guilty of breaking the commandment when we vote for tax cuts and "kickers" rather than strengthen programs against child abuse or extend health insurance to the 35 to 40 million Americans who are without it? Furthermore, we ignore the positive aspects of this commandment as we focus on individual sins, thus ignoring collective or social sins.

Law as a Schoolmaster

Clarification is needed. We speak of the law in two ways. According to Hans Schwarz, a German theologian, the law has a secular use as well as a theological use.[1] In the secular sense, he noted that the law "guards against serious transgressions and crimes and protects the public peace" and is applied through such authorities as parents and teachers "and also through secular, societal laws". He added that it is "possible for one to live within the framework of commonly accepted—secular—laws without becoming a lawbreaker". (Does this include running red traffic lights?) It is the

> second sense or use of the law, which Luther characterizes as the true use. Jesus illustrates this use of the law in his Sermon on the Mount [in which] he greatly intensified the will of God. A pure heart and perfect obedience are required of people before God... [Thus the law] has become unfulfillable. Instead, the law reveals to them and even intensifies their sinfulness.

The result is that such a view also intensifies our sense of guilt as we recognize that we are law breakers—not merely in the sense of specifics but in spirit and in our inability to rise above our nature. So the law pushes or prods us to seek the gospel. Thus Luther said that the law is a schoolmaster encouraging us to forgiveness and reconciliation with God through Jesus Christ. Theologian Schwarz wrote:

> In the reformed and pietistic streams of Protestantism, which seem to stress the obligating power of the gospel, one often hears the binding demands [laws] of the biblical message so much that the gospel is overshadowed and even obliterated. Luther sharply distinguished between law and gospel, but without separating one from the other. He stressed that the Word of God encounters human beings in the twofold form of law and gospel.[2]

How much of Protestantism (not just the right wing) has its focus on the individual, as evident in such expressions as "I give my heart to Jesus," "I make a decision for Christ," "I want" or "I need". The subject "I" is quite prominent. Along these lines, it appears that being

---

[1] Hans Schwarz, *True Faith in the True God: An Introduction to Luther's Life and Thought* (Augsburg Fortress), pp. 103-109. Schwartz teaches at the University of Regensburg, Germany. Following quotations are from this source.

[2] The term "Word of God" should not be understood simply as the Bible, a book, although it is through the printed page that the living Word comes to us. In the first chapter of John's Gospel, the "Word" is another name for Christ.

a Christian is within one's power and is a matter of controlling one's behavior (or being controlled). Clearly we need the distinctions of "law and gospel," as noted by Schwarz:

> Law and gospel have entirely different, even opposing functions. The law establishes what one should do and what one is not allowed to do, and as a consequence of human failure, it accuses and condemns. The gospel, on the other hand, has as its content God's promise in Christ... The Gospel preaches, therefore, the forgiveness of sins... The good news of Christ's saving work and the redemption from sin can neither be understood nor desired if one has not recognized the extent of human estrangement from God [as evident in] the law.

Distinguishing between law and gospel, it is also important to guard against narrow interpretations of morality. To imagine the religious right wing enforcing a moral code by using the power of government is to recall New England's witch hunts, the Spanish inquisition or current examples in Islamic states. Moreover, it is important to guard against moral positions which focus on the individual while ignoring social problems. The Lord's Prayer opens with "Our Father" not "My Father". Notice how these various aspects of law and gospel are brought together in the Confession at the opening of the Liturgy:

> we confess that we are in bondage to sin and cannot free ourselves. We have sinned against you...by what we have done and by what we have left undone. We have not loved you with our whole heart; we have not loved our neighbors as ourselves.

And then follows the word of forgiveness, personalized for us by the pastor.

A thoughtful conclusion:
   An old Scottish prayer: "Lord, grant that we are always completely in the right for we shall surely never change our minds". [3]

---

[3] Eric Gritsch, "From Servanthood to Serpenthood," *Dialog,* Summer 1998, p. 209.

5

Who is Guilty? Who Decides?

April 2, 1999

Monica and Iraq are ignored; the news is now focused on Serbia. But it's complicated. We see pictures of long lines of refugees and we know about heartless killings, tortures and disappearances. With the strength of a super-power and Nato, can the world stand by and do nothing? Sarajevo saw the opening of World War I and Sarajevo is in the news again at the end of the century. With a history of unrest, the roles of "good guys and bad guys" in the Balkans seem to be exchanged and traded every couple centuries. But the bloodshed continues.

This century has seen horrible assaults on humanity. In Cambodia two leaders of the Khmer Rouge have been held responsible for the deaths of 1.5 to 2 million but there has never been a trial. Up to a million people were slaughtered in Rwanda during four months of 1994. Earlier in the century there were the dislocations and killings of millions under Communist Stalin in the name of the left wing and the systematic killing of additional millions under Nazi Hitler in the name of the right wing.

In recent years at least 200,000 people were slaughtered in Bosnia but the western nations reacted very cautiously. Among the problems were the forming of acceptable definitions of crimes as well as matters of national sovereignty. David Fromkin, a professor of history and law at Boston University, described some of the problems, writing:

> In Rome on July 17, 1998, two-thirds of the world's countries signed a treaty establishing an international criminal court to deal with war crimes, genocide, aggression, and crimes against humanity... The United States refused to sign the Rome treaty... Yet at Nuremberg a half-century ago it committed itself to two other fundamental departures from traditional international law that the Rome treaty embodies. One of these is holding individuals responsible for actions taken by the states whose leaders they were... Then there are the new categories of crime: "war crimes" are straightforward and

traditional, clearly defined by The Hague and Geneva Conventions, but "aggression" is something else again. It is what each side claims the other side did. The same can be said about "crimes against humanity" and "crimes against the peace." [1]

The very title of Fromkin's article notes that international law is at the "frontiers". There are problems in defining the terms. For example, the word "genocide" was never officially used at Nuremberg and it has been noted that at the time it did not even appear in the Oxford English Dictionary. [2] Moreover, the concept of national sovereignty creates immense problems in dealing with international law. Fromkin noted that the planet is divided into about 200 political entities, each claiming to be fully independent and sovereign, i.e., "acknowledging no higher authority".

Consider an example: In Chile the dictator Augusto Pinochet came to power (with U.S. help) in 1973 but is accused of 3,197 deaths and disappearances of Chileans during his first two years in power. While in London for medical treatments, the Spanish judicial system requested that he be extradited to Spain for trial on charges of torturing and killing Spanish citizens. Awaiting a decision, he remains in London under house arrest. Few of us are specialized in such problems of international law. In fact, it is with some hesitancy that I choose this topic for my Musing. But the picture of a grieving parent in Chile or the burning images of suffering in the long lines of refugees cannot be put aside lightly.

It is increasingly clear that the world has become more unpredictable and more dangerous than it has been. And because of current complexities it is not enough to think of morality only in personal or individual terms. At a conference of Lutheran theologians on the subject of ethics, Richard Perry said:

> What I am concerned about is the support and complicity with structures that hurt people, and our own responsibility to challenge them and create structures that promote and enhance life and the common good.

---

[1] David Fromkin, "International Law at the Frontiers," *World Policy Journal*, Winter 1998-99, p. 59.

[2] Roy Gutman, "Bringing Genocide to Justice," *The Washington Spectator*, March 1, 1999. Backed by American University's Washington College of Law, Gutman and David Rieff are editing a publication to be called *Crimes of War: What the Public Should Know*.

The point is illustrated by another participant, Cynthia Moe-Lobeda, who said:

> [As a missionary in Central America] I have been seared by that experience, by encountering tortured people and realizing that my government supported the torturers, and by encountering deadly poverty and realizing that it was linked to the global economic order by which middle and upper strata North Americans benefit. I cannot escape knowing these things. [3]

In the article quoted above David Fromkin traced the "foreshadowing" of international law in various periods of time: the Roman Empire, Christendom in the middle ages, and a European order (1648-1914) which was broken at Sarajevo. At this time, without the assumed unity of Western and European civilization, but with the inclusion of diverse cultures and religions and nations, one can readily wonder about some higher authority. I would like to think that the responsibility of the United States does not rely simply on size and power. The bully in the school yard is not a desirable model but what should the model be?

With some 200 nation states all claiming sovereignty, none willing to recognize any higher authority, is there a place for an International Criminal Court? It has been said that the Human Rights Declaration of the United Nations came about not from government but because of public pressure. What will the public reaction be to more pictures of suffering refugees, three or more captive American soldiers or the discovery of more mass graves? Reflecting on massacres in Rwanda, Colette Braeckman, a Belgian journalist wrote:

> One asks oneself what the actual significance of these macabre statistics is... Finally one must have the lucidity to admit one's own puzzlement, revulsion, incomprehension, sympathy, empathy, and even exhaustion. [4]

Rodney King's question after being beaten by police in Los Angeles: Why can't we all get along?

---

[3] Karen Bloomquist and John Stumme (eds.), *The Promise of Lutheran Ethics*, (Fortress Press), 167, 153.

[4] Colette Braeckman, "Cowardice and Conscience," *World Policy Journal*, Winter 1998-99, p. 99.

6

Think Globally, Act Globally

May 10, 1999

Some years ago an acquaintance who liked to speak in grand terms said to me in all seriousness, "My philosophy is the pursuit of happiness". It was narrow and egocentric but at the time I had no response. However, now, many years later, I have an answer to that unforgotten statement, thanks to a guest at St. James. Last month Dr. William Foege, speaking at St. James, stated that there have been many attempts to define civilization. [1] One of these is happiness, which caused him to wonder whether a three-year-old might be more civilized than the parents.

Another approach, Dr. Foege added, might be related to how people treat each other. This would take seriously the parable of the Good Samaritan, which he described with a bumper sticker's quote to think globally, act locally". When he amended this by saying "think globally, act globally" my thoughts turned to the congregations I have served. In all of them there were dedicated people who recognized the importance of the parable and who would wholeheartedly support projects of aid in parish and community. But how difficult it was for each of these congregations to act globally. Now, as congregational budgets grow, the amounts used locally increase but unfortunately the dollars given for churchwide or international work diminish.

I wonder how many Lutherans can identify such acronyms as LWR and LWF, which stand for Lutheran World Relief and the Lutheran World Federation, two organizations which grew significantly after World War 2 in attempts to be Good Samaritans in the global scene. Through our international associations we have remarkable opportunities to be of assistance to people in need. The Lutheran World Federation, according to a recent report is "a communion of Lutheran Churches in all parts of the world" comprising 124 member churches in 69 countries, representing 57.6

---

[1] Dr. William Foege, the Hulda and Adam Koehler Memorial Lecture at St. James Lutheran Church, Portland, April 11, 1999. Dr. Foege is the Senior Health Policy Fellow, The Carter Center and Distinguished Professor of International Health at Emory University.

million of the world's 61 million Lutherans. [2] From its main office in Geneva, Switzerland, the LWF is "the churches' agent, acting on behalf of its members in areas of common interest such as ecumenical relations, theology, humanitarian assistance, human rights, communication and the various aspects of mission and development".

To illustrate, the LWF's Office for Ecumenical Affairs has been engaged in activities such as Anglican-Lutheran relations, Lutheran-Ro-man Catholic joint studies, as well as work on a Lutheran-Orthodox joint commission. It is clearly stated that "the theological core of the Lutheran Reformation is ecumenical in its nature".

The LWF's Department for World Service, for example, in addition to its continuing programs offers funding for emergency response, cooperating with local churches in 25 countries. For instance, this includes a field office in the former Yugoslavia. Beyond immediate relief this department has programs for long-term development in 22 different countries, such as soil and water projects, primary health care and sanitation. An intriguing program is that of income generation to help people get on their feet. For instance, "Yon Yiem, 35, a resident of Kam Por village in Cambodia...is a successful businesswoman who tells how with the help of LWF she started buying and selling mosquito nets... From the profits of her business, Mrs. Yiem has managed to pay back her loan to purchase a sewing machine".

Two members of St. James have offered examples of the LWF at work. Bob Metzger turned our attention to the efforts of the Lutherans in Vladivostok, Russia, to repair their church building, returned to the congregation after it's use as a naval museum. Marvis Gilnet, traveling in the Near East, visited the Church of the Redeemer in Jerusalem with its 12th-century chapel, Nativity (Christmas Church) in Bethlehem and the Lutheran Augusta Victoria Hospital on the Mount of Olives, all of which are closely related to the LWF. This hospital continues to be a major Christian presence in East Jerusalem as a hospital but also through programs for healthcare in the villages, vocational training and employment for the blind. In this hospital work the LWF has cooperated closely with the United Nations Relief and Works Agency and the Lutheran Church in Jordan.

Regarding "bridges between the local and the global," Sigrun Møgedal, treasurer of the LWF, wrote that

---

[2] *L W F Today,* March, 1998. Following quotations from this source. Address: Lutheran World Federation, P.O. Box 2100, CH-1211 Geneva 2, Switzerland.

> Member churches need the world communion, not only as an instrument to reach out or to receive resources, but in order to make sense of its own identity in a globalized world. [3]

Referring to the Augusta Victoria Hospital, Møgedal stated that

> All East Jerusalem institutions with a Palestinian identity...are facing financial crises, largely due to the political situation and the restrictions on movement. The hospital supports the legitimate rights of the Palestinians to be in Jerusalem. These institutions are now at the forefront of the struggle to preserve the multi-cultural and multi-religious nature of the city. Also for AVH, the identity as a Palestinian Christian institution in Jerusalem is seen as most critical.

As Lutherans at St. James, Portland, we have in effect joined hands with the Crusader Knights of St. John of the 12th century, known as the Hospitallers, who built a chapel and hospital in Jerusalem, with a Turkish Sultan who in 1869 made a gift of the chapel to the Prussian king, with Kaiser Wilhelm II who ordered a new church built in 1898 and with world-wide Christians who support Augusta Victoria Hospital and Redeemer Church which now houses Lutheran congregations worshiping in English, Arabic, German and Danish.

Referring back to Dr. Foege, he noted that there are many factors contributing to wholeness and health for both individuals and society, factors which include satisfying relations, opportunities for optimal health, responsibility for others, opportunities to develop positive abilities and purpose in life. Dr. Foege concluded that church and faith contribute to all of these. In stark contrast to many popular political positions which reflect the withering narrowness of a selfish pursuit of happiness, we can be grateful for opportunities in church and faith to express purpose in life.

---

[3] *L W F Documentation,* No. 43 (Geneva, December 1998), p. 132.

7

Structures for World Community

June 11, 1999

For most of us the life of a hermit or a loner is not a desirable goal but why is it that so many people reflect that goal? If they were to state a philosophy, it might well be some form of individualism which could be expressed as "me-first-ism". Yet as more and more people crowd our planet and increasing demands are placed on limited resources, the reality is finally dawning on us that the structures of life on this planet are fragile and cannot endlessly endure slash and burn tactics or ever expanding populations all dreaming about opulent or soap opera lifestyles.

In the face of this the number of states claiming nationhood or sovereignty is increasing. For example, will the Kosovo Liberation Army eventually achieve its goal of full independence for this state, thus turning it into another sovereign nation? But is self-interest—personal or national—always the best policy? It should be clear that on a personal level as well as an international level we must get along with one another.

With the news focused on Kosovo the United Nations has received increased attention. Recall that shortly after the devastation of World War II, the charter was signed on June 26, 1945, and in this brief history of fifty years the UN has had a turbulent time. During the Cold War only the USSR and a few of its allies would vote against some of its resolutions. A decade or two ago the tables turned and the holdouts were the United States and Israel. That was when we (the U.S.) petulantly decided not to pay our dues.

Anticipating the fiftieth anniversary of the United Nations, the Council of the Lutheran World Federation instructed the General Secretary to send a letter to the member churches, which stated the following:

> During its short and turbulent history the U N has become a powerful symbol of the unity of humankind. Created to be a forum for peacemaking and international understanding, the United Nations—with

all its shortcomings—nevertheless embodies some of the great visions that the Church has carried through the centuries. As Christians we can affirm the United Nations' Charter, which states the determination of its members "to reaffirm faith in fundamental human rights, in the dignity and worth of the human person". [1]

For an organization in which all its members claim to be sovereign, there are many problems in building the structures intended to serve such large purposes as the securing of global peace, justice and human rights. Challenges are obvious with "the effects of poverty, famine and environmental decay, nuclear proliferation, the shift of power within and between industrial countries, the breakup of multinational states, and religious and ethnic conflicts".

At a symposium to discuss the role of religion in shaping the future of the United Nations, Dr. Christopher Joyner, professor of international law at Georgetown University, noted that "it is easy to be critical about the United Nations, ...easy to cite disappointments and failures" but on the other hand with so much

> UN-bashing it is also easy to forget the many important things that the United Nations has accomplished... Though stymied by diplomatic gridlock during the Cold War, the United Nations did help mitigate the ideological conflict... Keep in mind, too, that as old empires disintegrated...the United Nations eased the birth of resultant states into the international community, ...more than 130 new independent states. Keep in mind also that the United Nations won five Nobel Peace Prizes: in 1988 the Blue Helmet Peacekeepers...in 1965 UNICEF [Children Emergency Fund], in 1954 and again in 1981... [work with refugees and in 1969 with international labor].
>
> We are also quick to forget that many functional programs of the United Nations have been successful. Perhaps most outstanding has been that of the World Health Organization which wiped out smallpox and has nearly eradicated river blindness (the scourge of West Africa). And WHO is playing the leading role in combating AIDS across the world... The point here plainly evident: The United Nations *has* made a difference in bettering the human condition... [2]

---

[1] *LWF Documentation No. 35*, 18-28 June 1994, (Lutheran World Federation, Geneva, Switzerland), pp. 96-98.

[2] Dr. Christopher Joyner, "Rethinking the Troubled Partnership," *The United Nations after 50: The Role of Religion in Shaping its Future*, the 22nd Annual Symposium on Politics and Ethics, (Oct. 26, 1995, The Luther Institute, Washington, D.C.), 47-52.

Structures for World Community

Questions Dr. Joyner raised can "sharpen appreciation" of the value of our participation in the United Nations:

> First, is the world a safer, more secure stable place with a functioning United Nations?
> Second, what would the world be like without the United Nations?
> Third, are U.S. interests well served by having a functioning United Nations and by actively participating in UN matters?

Although the United Nations is a political organization, it merits the encouragement and support of the Church in so many "issues on the world community's agenda," as noted in the letter from the LWF's General Secretary. Further, "the problems of a lack of cohesion of governing structures and the erosion of participation in and respect for political systems" point to the need for building structures through which diverse people can live securely on this planet. Those who have nothing good to say about government (the bashers) should be reminded that the alternative to government is anarchy and there is no safety (even for the rich) in such a jungle. Moreover, in the words of Senator Paul Simon (Ill.):

> As people of faith, we have no option. We cannot be the ones who walk by on the other side of the road. If we want our children and grandchildren to live in a world of peace and security, we must act together today.[3]

Let's pay our share of the UN dues and work with others to build an effective structure.

---

[3] Rev. Dr. Paul Wee, "Summary and Conclusions," *The United Nations After 50*, (The Luther Institute), p. 55.

8

Understanding 1492 and 1969

July 24, 1999

The story of the Kennedy tragedy has dominated the news recently—understandably so, because that family has had a significant place in our national history.[1] JFK and Camelot are bitter-sweet stories, but it occurs to me that the individual selfishness and cynicism of our days could benefit from the inspiration of President Kennedy's "Ask not what the country can do for you but what you can do for your country".

Another bit of recent news did not have the headlines but did remind us of an event which might be far more significant. This was the 30th anniversary of human footsteps on the moon, an event in 1969 which galvanized the attention of the world. For example, Mexico issued some postage stamps with the word "luna" imposed very simply on a footprint. But having won the Russian space challenge and kept President Kennedy's promise to set foot on the moon, our country has lost interest in space.

I wonder however, how this century will be remembered centuries hence. Think back: what happened in the 1400s? A few staunch Lutherans might say that Martin Luther was born in1486 whereas most answers would probably state that in 1492 Columbus sailed the ocean blue. Nevertheless in the days of Columbus Europeans were not interested in the discoveries of a new world and the most interesting news in Spain was not Columbus, who became almost a discard, but the expulsion of the Muslims and Jews in 1492. Will 1969 in the future have even greater impact than 1492?

What about this century? There have been books and television programs and undoubtedly there will be much more by the end of the year. Peter Jennings co-authored a book and narrated a

---

[1] For those of us who are interested in flying, it is also sad to see the spotlight of criticism focused on accidents in aviation, with questions regarding the percentage of accidents caused by pilot error and the call for regulations to prevent more accidents. One might also ask how many of the 41,000 deaths every year in auto accidents are caused by driver error. What should be done—add regulations in flying but raise the highway speed limits and smile at those who run the red lights?

television series which focused on the century's highlights. John Ikenberry wrote several book reviews of attempts to view the century. [2] According to Ikenberry, Robert Dahl's political views in *On Democracy* showed that

> Although the world has seen many democratic gains, democratic government has collapsed and given way to authoritarian rule more than 70 times this century. The creation of democratic government does not rest solely on institutional design but on democratic culture and traditions.

These words are warning to us that our country's traditional democratic strength should not be taken for granted. The current wave of short-sighted self-interest, cynical views of government, the unwillingness to strengthen education, and our indifference to the have-nots are the seeds of dissension—and revolution. Ikenberry next wrote that Clive Ponting in The Twentieth Century "seeks to paint a more general portrait of the century, tackling themes such as the environment, globalization, societal change, empire, freedom, fascism, and revolution," noting the "struggle in everyday life between progress and degradation." He concluded that Ponting's view is overly pessimistic, "anticipating a world based on progress for the few and barbarism for the many". More optimistic, on the other hand, is Martin Gilbert, *A History of the Twentieth Century*, "which portrays the bloody battles of this century as a triumph for democracy and the rule of law". Ikenberry concluded that "the century may be ending, but the contest over its history is just beginning".

It would be helpful to consider another contest. A couple hundred years ago, when there were celebrations of the 300th anniversary of Columbus's discovery, a French philosopher (Abbé Raynal) offered a prize for the best answer to this question: "Has the discovery of America been beneficial or harmful to the human race?" [3] Describing this event, David B. Davis and Steven Mints in *The Boisterous Sea of Liberty* noted:

---

[2] John Ikenberry, *Foreign Affairs* 78:3 (May-June 1999), pp. 133-134, book reviews: Robert Dahl, *On Democracy* (Yale 1999); Clive Ponting, *The Twentieth Century*, (Henry Holt, 1999), and Martin Gilbert, *A History of the Twentieth Century* (Wm. Morrow, 1999).

[3] David B. Davis and Steven Mints (eds.), *The Boisterous Sea of Liberty* (Oxford University Press, 1998), p. 37.

> Eight responses to the question survive. Of these, four argued that Columbus's voyage had harmed human happiness. The European discovery of the New World had a devastating impact on the Indian peoples of the Americas. Oppressive labor, disruption of the Indian food supply, deliberate campaigns of extermination, and especially disease decimated the Indian population... Within a century of contact the Indian population in the Caribbean and Mexico had shrunk by more than 90%.

During the sixteenth century the Hapsburg Empire included Spain, Austria, Italy, Holland and much of the New World and during that time "Spain's enemies created an enduring set of ideas known as the 'Black Legend,'" in which the Spanish were marked as cruel and corrupt people.

This causes me to wonder how people in other parts of the world a couple centuries from now will view the United States. It is obvious that the Statue of Liberty's motto no longer reflects national attitudes. If there has been a national theme for this century, it has been a negativism—to be against communism. But what have we been for? With the collapse of our enemy, is it fair to say that we are in disarray, scrambling in a power struggle for "I want mine and I want it now"? Is it possible to develop a vision of an America with a positive goal that is not self-serving?

In our national life there have leaders with great vision, such as George Washington, Abraham Lincoln, Franklin Delano Roosevelt, Daniel Webster, Theodore Roosevelt. One historian, Michael Lind, has written that these great statesmen all had one thing in common: they were Hamiltonians, that is they agreed with the vision of Alexander Hamilton. [4] The major author of the Federalist Papers, George Washington's aide, and the first Secretary of the Treasury, Hamilton envisioned a unified industrialized nation with economic and military strength in contrast to Jeffersonians who preferred an isolationist, rural America of strong states and a weak federal government. It is clear that as we approach the end of the century the debate continues. We can hope that through this debate a vision for our life together will be formed. As people of faith we have a responsibility to take part in this debate.

---

[4] Michael Lind, *Hamilton's Republic* (Free Press, 1997). He is also the author of *Up From Conservatism*.

9

Our Brother's Keeper

September 6, 1999

A radio commentator noted, as I recall, that a decade ago the average executive of a business had an income about ten times the average worker in his company whereas now the average income for a CEO is about 400 times that of the worker. And the local newspaper had an alarming report that the gap between rich and poor has grown into an "economic chasm". The chasm is so wide that the richest 2.7 million Americans, the top 1 %, will have "as many after-tax dollars to spend as the bottom 100 million". [1] Many Americans who struggle with budgets vote for tax-cutting measures not realizing that in the last couple decades the greatest tax cuts have benefited the very rich and the middle class is diminished.

One can understand theoretically that economic disparities lead to unrest among voters but countering policies of greed is also the biblical concern of being our brother's keeper. Christine Grumm, formerly the vice-president of the Evangelical Lutheran Church in America and now with the Lutheran World Federation, addressed a church leaders' consultation in Geneva on the theme of working for a common future. [2] She wrote that as we look ahead we do so from widely differing perspectives, noting examples from the words of Jesus in Matthew 25:

I was hungry
- for many of us these are words uttered between breakfast in the morning and the noonday meal.
- for the child who has not been fed for days because of famine these words may be the beginning of the end of his/her life.

I was thirsty
- for people living in Geneva that means going to the tap and getting a glass of water.

---

[1] David C. Johnston, New York Times, *The Oregonian*, Sept. , 1999.

[2] Christine Grumm, "Are we willing to risk a common future together?" *LWF Documentation*, No. 35 (Sept. 1994, Lutheran World Federation, Geneva).

- up until a few months ago for the people of Sarajevo that meant risking one's life by dodging sniper bullets to fetch water from the one pump still working.

I was a stranger
- that may have been how some of you felt yesterday at the beginning of this consultation.
- for millions of people around the world it has meant being forced to leave their homes and families to become refugees, often...where they are neither welcomed nor accepted.

I was sick
- for some that has meant having a bad cold or the flu.
- for others it has been the diagnoses of AIDS or another terminal illness that brings with it an almost certain death sentence.

So you see how Jesus' words take on drastically different meanings when applied to various situations. Yet, these words... call on each of us, as we share in the pain and suffering of one another, to take care of our brother or sister in need as if we were serving Christ himself.

The focus in recent decades has been on the individual, which is to say that the focus has become self-centered or selfish. This is evident in government—What can government do for me? It is also evident in religion as in churches which emphasize a theology focused on the individual—My needs, my good feelings. On the other hand, a theology based on God's grace coming to us through Word and Sacrament, makes it clear that God is at the center and in such a perspective we find ourselves related to our brothers and sisters. Russell Sadler, a writer in Ashland, Oregon, wrote:

> At no time in this century has the Judeo-Christian ethic of being our brother's keeper been so overwhelmed by the crass selfishness of accumulated wealth... Fundamentalist Protestant pastors preach a political gospel conspicuously lacking any semblance of Christian charity. Secular political leaders insist government "give charity a chance" [and so free themselves of responsibility] to meet the needs of the unfortunate... No serious reading of Scripture absolves us of the milleniums-old command to be our brother's and sister's keeper... For many self-styled conservatives and libertarians the poor are out of sight, out of mind...—a low-wage disposable work force that serves those who can still afford to live well. [3]

---

[3] Russell Sadler, "Reasons to care for each other," *The Daily Astorian*, Nov. 26, 1998.

Immediate reactions to the widening gap or chasm are likely to be personal or individual. However, the concern for brothers and sisters must recognize the complexity of the problem in its global reach. Consider the population explosion. A trivia item in the newspaper noted that "If the population of China walked past you in single file, the line would never end because of the rate of reproduction". After reading about U.S. population figures I estimated that by the time my grandchildren are 65 the population of this country will have doubled.

James Speth, administrator of the United Nations Development Program, wrote that "economic declines inevitably translate into political instability and social unrest". He added that "true development requires profound institutional changes... It entails investing in the human, social, environmental, and physical assets of the poor". [4] Speth then listed a number of countries showing the percentage of the population earning less that $1 a day, including the following: Zambia 85, Guatemala 53, India 53, Honduras 47, Brazil 24. Many human emergencies necessarily draw our attention, such as national and regional conflicts, terrorism, drugs, diseases, and environmental deterioration. However, Speth noted, these stem from poverty, inequity, joblessness and social deterioration. The highest motivation should not be the avoidance of personal or national trouble but concern for others in the human family. Such an attitude, for example, is not evident in the following item.

> Why should Greenwich, Conn., one of our advantaged communities, have one of the nation's highest percentage of learning-disabled students? Nearly 30 percent of its high school students are enrolled in special education. This is more than double the national average. It seems that once a student is classified as learning disabled, he or she becomes entitled to such goodies as one-on-one tutoring, untimed tests, and additional time to complete assignments. They also...get to take untimed SAT's. These kids have parents smart enough and cynical enough to manipulate the system to their advantage. Where does this leave the kids who really need help and who don't have such parents? [5]

To be our brother's keeper is more than giving a Christmas basket.

---

[4] James G. Speth, "The Plight of the Poor," *Foreign Affairs*, May-June 1999, 13-16.

[5] Charles Peters, "Tilting at Windmills," *Washington Monthly*, April 1999, p. 6.

10

Labels: Liberal and Conservative

October 4, 1999

A story I heard from my father concerned the first visit with his prospective in-laws on their farm in northern Illinois. Father wanted to make a good impression and at one point in the conversation proudly stated that he had just acquired a life insurance policy–remember that this was some years ago–to which his prospective father-in-law sternly stated: "Young man, you should learn how to stand on your own two feet. Insurance is socialism".

And so it is. But how strange that as our words and labels change meanings we frequently fail to clarify them. Handy political or ideological labels have broken down, becoming meaningless without definition. On the one hand, by "conservative" it was generally accepted that one wanted to preserve existing institutions or values, maintain a moderate point of view and resist rapid change. But this definition would not apply to many of the conservatives, religious or otherwise, now agitating in the Republican party. For example, consider the numerous efforts to amend the national constitution proposed by conservatives who appear not to want to conserve. On the other hand, the word "liberal" comes from a root meaning liberation or freedom, that an individual might be free of regulation. Nevertheless, liberals of this age have often been the ones who would use government to change social structures, as for example in the struggle against racism, in the development of social security or even (some decades back) such programs as rural electrification— hardly liberation from regulation.

The labels of political parties often contradict the terms "liberal" and "conservative". Other labels which have been subject to abuse are those which refer to a social or political "right wing" and "left wing". Many of us resist identification with the extremes of either the right or left wing in political thought. As a nation in World War II we fought the extremes of the "right" (Mussolini's Fascism and Hitler's Nazism) and in the Cold War we fought the extremes of the "left" (Stalinist Communism). Although in the last several decades

Labels: Liberal and Conservative

national energy and much money was dedicated against (leftist) Communism, it can be argued that from the '60s to the '80s there has been more danger from the political right than from the left. [1] This was certainly evident in Latin America, although there has been a significant swing to democracy in the last couple decades. In this country the danger on the right was especially noticeable in Richard Nixon's subversion of the Constitution, often in the name of "national security," the excuse used so frequently in Latin America. If the extremes of the left and of the right are identical in that they both produce authoritarian or totalitarian results, then it appears desirable to stand in the middle ground. But how difficult it is to find that middle and on close examination, is that middle truly desirable?

Consider a view of liberalism. It is difficult today to imagine the despair and the hopelessness prevalent in the 1930s. During a time of economic misery in America, Stalin was murdering millions of peasants and in 1933 Hitler took office. Many thoughtful people wondered whether democracy would survive against those strong political systems. It was said that these strong movements were all "anti-liberal" and that "democracy was insufficiently dynamic" to survive. There were both "rightists" and "leftists" in those days who argued that Roosevelt should take extraordinary or authoritarian powers. Instead, according to one historian, Fred Siegel,

> Roosevelt seized on [the word] liberal, until then a word of minor importance in the American political vocabulary, to describe his New Deal, his attempt to temper economic individualism with social democratic safeguards. For millions of Americans those safeguards—such as Social Security and bank deposit insurance—would become synonymous with the liberalism they repeatedly supported at the ballot box. [2]

Following World War II liberalism benefited many families through programs such as the G.I. bill and veterans' mortgages but by the 1960s it was in retreat, having lost much support of the middle class which it had helped develop.

Consider also a view of conservatism. Republicans have dreamed about bringing religious, social and economic conservatives

---

[1] It has been said that the USSR ceased to be a political model in the early 1970s because of the dismal example of its protégé Ethiopia.

[2] Fred Siegel, "Liberalism," *Reader's Companion to American History* (Houghton Mifflin Co., 1991), 653 ff. Following quotations are from this source.

together in one family but the unity appears artificial and the divisions are significant. Reagan's presidency has been considered the high point of conservatism in this century, but there have been voices of criticism from conservatives, such as George Will, who stated that in America "there are almost no conservatives, properly understood". Historian Siegel offers this description:

> In Europe conservatism was based on hereditary classes; in America it was based on hereditary religious, ethnic, and racial groups... To be a conservative, then, was to share in a religiously ordained vision of a largely stateless society of self-regulating individuals. This civil religion, preached by President Herbert Hoover, was shattered by the Great Depression... Conservatism triumphed [in later decades] because New Deal liberalism was unable to accommodate the new cultural and political demands unleashed by the civil rights revolution, feminism, and the counterculture, all of which was exacerbated by the Kulturkampf over Vietnam.

Obviously, the terms "liberal" and "conservative" need definition, if we are to speak with any precision. Carrying liberalism to an extreme is to believe in the essential goodness of human nature. Pressing conservatism (in current views) to extreme, we see the robber barons. Moreover, the extremes of right and left can meet in dictatorship or totalitarianism. We should therefore remain critical, understanding that theologically we recognize the sinfulness of humanity and all of its structures.

There is a problem, however, if we seek only to avoid the extremes by standing in the middle, as posed by an eminent authority:

> The Church Mouse once delivered an aphorism pertinent here: "If you stand in the middle of the road, the traffic in two directions will flatten you into road kill." [3]

---

[3] *Dialog, A Journal of Theology*, Vol. 34, No. 1, p. 6 – probably from the pen of Ted Peters.

11

Classrooms without festivals?

December 20, 1999

Can you imagine what a school teacher would do without special celebrations? How could the teacher decorate the classroom without Thanksgiving and pilgrims, Halloween and goblins, Valentine's Day? Of course, we must be careful about Christmas but we can have Rudolph and Santa and chimneys. Both teachers and students need this round of celebrations just as some people use birthdays and anniversaries. I would like to ignore my birthday but others in the family obviously take pleasure in reminding me of my mortality. Nevertheless, we all do benefit from the round of festivals and observances. In this regard, what a marvelous invention we have in the Church Year, the sequence of celebrations: Advent, Christmas, Epiphany, Lent, Palm Sunday, Holy Week, Easter, Ascension, Pentecost, Trinity, All Saints', Christ the King. The high points, of course, are Christmas, Easter and Pentecost.

Subjected at this time to the barrage of Christmas advertising, it's not difficult to lash out against the commercialization of Christmas. Over the years some of my sermons have indeed included critical comments about such excesses. However, I have often wondered what Christmas would be like without commercialization. Would it be like Pentecost, which theoretically ranks with Easter and Christmas but is generally ignored? Perhaps it would be helpful in church attendance if Pentecost were commercialized. Any ideas?

This raises questions regarding the battle lines between worship and culture. How does one affect the other? Ted Peters, editor of a theological journal, writing on ideological wars over culture and worship, stated that

> Pluralism means war... We are left with a culture devoid of a center, devoid of a common set of fundamental beliefs and values that bind us together as a people. Gone are the ultimates. Gone are the universals. Gone is the social glue, the sense of shared meaning.

With pluralism we can neutralize the festivals, substituting Santa Claus for the Christ child and greet one another not with "Merry Christmas" but with the secular "Happy Holidays," which is politically correct and proper even for those who have no religion. Is it possible to make use of the secular greeting where it is appropriate without admitting that the least common denominator should be our standard? Does a pluralistic culture invalidate religious expression?

Theologian Ted Peters suggested that for the Christian faith there are three possible strategies, which are to advance, retreat, or "swallow the Trojan horse". To advance, he wrote, would be to proclaim the Christian gospel as universally valid and to make the proclamation both inside the church and "in the public square". To retreat would be to separate the church from the public arena. The Trojan horse strategy "would be to turn the church itself into a naked public square, to ape the surrounding culture by giving up any sense of center and swallowing pluralism whole." [1]

One of the battle fronts identified by Peters was worship and curiously it was located within the church. With a strategy for advance, one position holds that liturgical renewal should be taken seriously, that the integrity of the liturgy be respected. He noted that worship should move "from a private religious experience to a public identity in Christ [as] a movement that bridges the personal and public dimensions of our lives".

An opposite view is held by those who use "entertainment evangelism". Here Peters quoted the pastor of the Lutheran Community Church of Joy, in Glendale, Arizona:

> Entertainment-oriented churches are growing... When people come to Community Church of Joy on Sunday morning, they have fun. We may have a stage band, comedians, clowns, dramas, mini concerts and productions, high energy choreography, as well as many other entertainment forms. [2]

This may be an extreme example, but one does not have to visit many churches without recognizing entertainment features on Sunday morning, often cheap imitations of television talk shows. In some cases the altar as focal point gives way to a roving emcee with a microphone. Peters' conclusion is that the battle within the church is

---

[1] Ted Peters, "Culture Wars: Should Lutherans Volunteer to be Conscripted?" *Dialog* 32:1 (Winter 1993), 37.

[2] Peters, "Culture Wars," 37 ff. Further quotations are from this source.

Classrooms without festivals?

"not only enervating, it is self-destructive". I, for one, like his comment that "entertainment along with its accompanying individualism and pragmatism loses the biblically based order and symbolic involvement of the classic Christian worship pattern".

For about three decades there has been a swing toward religion that is individualistic and emotional. When the focus is on "my needs, my feelings, my happiness" there is little need for an altar with a cross which symbolize the presence of a self-sacrificing God. To respect the integrity of the liturgy, one does not have to follow the book mechanically, but the encounter of a people with God should be noted in definite progression: a humble entrance (confession), words of praise to God, listening to the Word (Scripture, psalmody, sermon), a response (offering of self, gifts and petitions) and then being strengthened with the Bread of life.

A swing to individualistic and emotional forms of worship has been noticeable in each of several centuries. In the 18th century (about 1740 -) it was called the Great Awakening. In the next century it was called the Second Awakening, known by many as the time of tent revivals and the sawdust trail. This was broken off by the Civil War. In our 20th century the movement is not easily defined but it has been significant in the last several decades. Has the trend peaked?

If this were a sermon, I would suggest that you turn to the Preface on p. 6 of the Lutheran Book of Worship and take note of the first paragraph:

> Corporate worship expresses the unity of the people of God and their continuity with Christians across the ages. In the liturgical tradition are the gestures, songs, and words by which Christians have identified themselves and each other. The Lutheran Confessions set our liturgical life within that mainstream of Christian worship: "We do not abolish the Mass but religiously keep and defend it... We keep traditional liturgical forms" (Apology to the Augsburg Confession, 24).

It occurs to me that a proper conclusion to this page would be the words written on each manuscript by the second most famous Lutheran (Johann Sebastian Bach):

Soli Deo Gloria.

12

Lutherans in London

January 30, 2000

For a couple weeks this month Sandra and I had a full schedule of stage plays in London and Stratford-on-Avon. We were part of a tour for students interested in literature and drama from Pacific University. Intended for students, the accommodations were not plush but the price was right. Open also to the community, we did not have to keep a journal or write critiques of the plays. Ten plays were on our schedule in addition to tours backstage and meeting with actors. Some plays were old (Antony and Cleopatra) and some were modern (Three Days of Rain). We enjoyed the entire tour, but I'd like to mention a couple thought-provoking talks.

One sad bit of conversation occurred during intermission at a play when I purchased some ice cream from a vendor at the head of an aisle in the theater. Unwrapping the package I asked where I might dispose of the wrapping and he said it should be dropped on the floor. I objected to this but he took the wrapper from my hand and indeed dropped it behind him with a comment that it would provide additional employment. I then asked if he himself might have that additional work in cleaning but he was clearly incensed by the question, responding with "No, do you think I'm Mexican?" Unable to think of a proper response, I simply said that I did not think that was funny. Some time later the thought occurred to me that I should have responded to him in Spanish and with a slip of the tongue say that I was Mexican (instead of Puerto Rican).

One of the modern plays, whose title I don't care to promote, was terribly depressing. With a setting in Dublin, there were only three actors, the principal one being markedly deprived in vocabulary—every other word was foul—and a context which was either depraved or at least deprived of hope. Sandra's comment was that we did not need to spend a full evening listening to the meanderings of a drunken Irishman. But one couple in our group, both school teachers, said they enjoyed the play, defending their opinion with the thought that the play's theme was one of redemption.

Lutherans in London

It was interesting that this couple, who stated that they were "not Christians," were the only ones who referred to the play with a term often used theologically. I would argue that redemption was clearly a need but the focus or emphasis of the play was the depressing human condition which it portrayed. The story appeared "to sell" on the predicament, not redemption. Speaking of redemption, this play was a far cry from the theological themes evident in C. S. Lewis' marvelous Lion, Witch and Wardrobe, which we saw at the magnificent theater in Stratford-on-Avon, the finale of the tour.[1]

During this visit to London the National Gallery had a special exhibit on Botticelli's "Mystic Nativity," which was described as reflecting the painter's twin interests in theology, the incarnation and eschatology. The Gallery may have scheduled this exhibit at this time because of the current turning of the century (millennium) and in Botticelli's time the year 1500 appeared ominous as a time for doomsday. Thus, in his painting of the Nativity he devoted an upper portion to angels carrying off some people to heaven whereas in the lower portion he painted seven demons (for the seven deadly sins) crawling out of fissures in the earth. The central feature of the painting, the Madonna and Child, represented the incarnation. It occurs to me that a U.S. postage stamp for Christmas a few years back featured Botticelli's Madonna and Child.

On our own at the National Gallery, Sandra and I were fascinated by a cartoon (draft outline) by Leonardo which was never painted. Quite large, it occupied one wall of a darkened alcove. We sat on a bench by the opposite wall to relate a printed description to what we saw. Titled "The Virgin and Child with St. Anne and St. John the Baptist" by Leonardo da Vinci (d. 1519), it was charcoal, black and white on tinted paper. Mary was seated (leaning) on the lap of Anne, her mother. The Child (an infant) was held by Mary and was facing John, an older child, who was leaning up against them. To us this appeared to be an unusual configuration.

On a Sunday morning we took the underground to St. Paul's, emerging in time to hear the bells and then wandered up to St. Anne's Lutheran Church, proceeding to get lost within the three blocks. St. Anne's is an international congregation, founded in 1951 and is part of the Lutheran Church in Great Britain and the Lutheran World Federation. Sandra and I have visited St. Anne's on previous

---

[1] Sandra was reluctant to see this play because she was afraid that the visual imagery would damage the greater imagination possible from print—and she had read the book numerous times. However, after seeing the play, she was delighted with it.

occasions, always enjoying the international aspect. During World War II, just in Great Britain, Lutheran services of worship on a scheduled basis were offered in 22 languages. Now, for example, St. Anne's currently holds services in Amharic (Ethiopia) and Swahili (East Africa) languages as well as English. For a small congregation, it also enjoys a high reputation for its musical program, as described in its Sunday bulletin:

> St. Anne's is known for its music, particularly in the Lutheran tradition of Bach, Telemann, and Buxtehude. St. Anne's Music Society, a registered charity which is part of [the]... Church, organizes more than 100 concerts and musical services each year. The Lecosaldi Ensemble, a group of professional musicians directed by Cantor Peter Lea-Cox, is based at the church.

The church building of St. Anne and St. Agnes is on permanent loan to the Lutherans by the Anglican (U.S.–Episcopal) Church and this building has a fascinating history, which dates from about 1150. As noted in the Sunday bulletin:

> The medieval church was destroyed in 1548 by a fire so severe that, in the words of a contemporary there was "nothynge left stondynge but the walles." It was rebuilt but again destroyed in the Great Fire of London in 1666. A new church, designed by Sir Christopher Wren was consecrated in 1680. ... The church suffered extensively in World War II but was restored following Wren's design. It was reconsecrated in 1966 and Lutheran congregations have used the church ever since. Famous residents in the parish have included John Milton, Jon Bunyan, and John Wesley... Why St. Anne, the grandmother of Jesus and St. Agnes, a thirteen-year old martyr of Rome, are linked in the church's name is a mystery.

Worshiping at St. Anne's, I thought of some similarities with St. James in Portland—both are small congregations but they both respect the liturgical heritage and both have broad vision. [2] Once again I was reminded of our partnership through the Lutheran World Federation.

---

[2] During coffee hour we were welcomed by Pr. Schmiege, (Moose Jaw, Sask.), Ass't Pr. Barnabas (Ethiopia) and Dr. Angela Kilmartin (sp. ?), an author who had been in Portland, Or., for her book promotions. I worried that my lack of literary understanding would be revealed but was much relieved when we learned that she was the author of books on urinary infections. Thus my literary ignorance might go unnoticed.

13

Worship and the Arts

February 14, 2000

On the afternoon of Superbowl Sunday Sandra and I went to the symphony where, incidentally, we heard Norman Leyden comment on the Schnitzer's full house on "Hyperbowl" Day. Without rushing, we were back at home in time to see a portion of the half-time extravaganza and I watched a portion of the game. I was disappointed to see that it was played in an enclosed dome after hearing the woeful weather reports. Sadness over the weather probably reflected the merchandisers rather than the players. But just think how exciting and unpredictable the game would have been had it been played in snow and icy slush. Moreover, the players might have earned their bonuses.

It was the spectacular half-time which turned my thoughts to patterns of worship. Really! Back in my seminary days general attitudes were turned against any sense of showmanship or theatrics. Many of us, myself included, took the ritual liturgy for granted, focusing primarily on the sermon and we gave little thought to the arts as reflections or expressions of faith, whether in vestments, music, stained glass or the structure of the building. This changed for me and for others with the growing appeal of the liturgical movement, which claimed that words and actions in use by the faithful over many centuries could continue to carry meaning when used purposefully. Moreover, the arts could also proclaim the faith.

In the late 1950s Billy Graham was becoming quite popular, dressed in coat and tie on an empty stage. In following decades evangelicalism was on the rise with a focus on the biblical sermon. Many envious Lutherans adopted folksy and casual styles of worship but their clumsy attempts could never compete with the Baptists. There were also those who argued that energy and money spent on worship and church buildings would be better spent on social causes. One growing congregation in New England decided to continue to rent a hall for worship and to dedicate the building fund to various causes. Plain and simple was the theme in worship.

But another trend appeared, which might be called "entertainment worship". Former accusations against pomp and ceremony in worship were forgotten as showmanship was on the rise, ever more ostentatious to keep up with Tammy Faye Baker's make-up and hair styles and to pay for the entertainer's diamond rings and possibly also to show that with Jesus one is happy (note the perpetual smile) and successful (meaning rich) —notwithstanding the original cross of Jesus. The roving emcee with a microphone replaced the pulpit and altar and the cross–hardly a symbol of success and positive thinking—was not much in evidence. Mega-churches were built and the pastor of a very large one near Detroit stated unabashedly that this (his?) church was begun after surveys in the area determined what people would like. Theology by the polls.

Some Lutherans (clergy and lay) have been so envious of the apparent success of evangelicalism and entertainment worship that they have virtually abandoned their heritage in a rush to adopt other styles. For example, some congregations have discarded altar and pulpit, disregarding their symbolic representation of Word and Sacrament. One theologian has said that "desperate clergy, pressured to be successful and beguiled by 'experts' with quick fixes," have rebelled against the centuries-old liturgy, as in the Lutheran Book of Worship. Many of the classic hymns by Isaac Watts and Charles Wesley as well as the Lutheran chorales have been replaced by sentimental texts and tunes which would be appropriate around a camp fire.

One writer has wondered whether it is even possible to speak of worship in a form "authentic to the Lutheran perception of faith, given the "diversity, indeed the confusion, of our self-perception". He quoted Evelyn Underhill's statement concerning the Lutheran approach, that "Luther did not seek to be an innovator in worship but to restore the ancient Christian balance between Word and Sacrament". [1]

In the mail I received a copy of a magazine from my alma mater with an article observing the significance of the Chapel of the Resurrection to Valparaiso University during the last 40 years—I graduated prior to its construction. Aside from its size (the largest university chapel in the country), it is an impressive building and in its use there has been a deliberate emphasis on the arts. The article, written by Gail McGrew Eifrig who first entered the chapel as a student, offered these impressions:

---
[1] Hans Boehringer, "Identity of Lutheran Worship," *Dialog* 16:4 (Fall 1977), pp. 287-291. Boehringer was writing in reference to the *Lutheran Book of Worship*, new at that time.

> Daughter of a pious Lutheran family that had been involved for years in mission starts in American Legion halls and community youth centers, I longed for the experience of God's house which would speak of the sublime. I wanted to worship in a place where awe for the majesty and wonder of God did not have to be wholly imagined, but instead could be experienced to some degree in a real, physical way. When I first went into the not-quite finished chapel in 1958, the building spoke powerfully to me of the presence of God. After a lifetime of experience there, it still does. [2]
>
> When the building was dedicated, in September of 1959, the [University president, O. P.] Kretzmann vision was in high gear. There was pomp and ceremony at a level that few Lutherans had ever experienced, with processions going around the outside, candlebearers and crossbearers, incense, choirs chanting in Latin, and a variety of liturgical garb, which only since then has become almost commonplace in Lutheran congregations.

This might all be considered empty pomp, unless the forms can carry meaning. But ceremonial or ritual activity is part of our lives. Notice the rituals in sports from the manner a high school basket ball team enters the floor to the spectacle of the Superbowl. And recall the lengthy opening ceremonials of the Olympics when the commentators in hushed tones reminded us of the old traditions of the Greeks. Ceremonial which is old and traditional can indeed be empty ritual but on the other hand it can carry meaning. Phrases of the liturgy may be mouthed mechanically, but they may carry weight for people today as they have in centuries past. Consider the Lord's Prayer. Empty ritual? –not necessarily. Eifrig describes a vision in worship:

> Kretzmann had a belief that a university chapel, based loosely on some models of European origins, could provide worship in which intellect, senses, and spirit would all be engaged together in praise and prayer and proclamation.

The liturgy, the building, the arts are not necessary for faith but they take us away from preoccupation with self and point us to the awesome majesty of God.

---

[2] Gail McGrew Eifrig, "Let us go into the house of the Lord," *Valpo* (The magazine of Valparaiso University) 16:1 (Winter 1999-2000). Eifrig is editor of Valparaiso University's *Cresset*. The following quotations are from this source.

14

Episcopalians and Lutherans

April 19, 2000

A significant gathering took place at St. James in Portland, Oregon, in 1988 when the presiding bishops of the Episcopal Church and the Evangelical Lutheran Church in America participated in a Eucharistic Service under the title "Implications of the Gospel". Bishops Edmond Browning and Herbert Chilstrom were leading their churches in directions established previously, as in the 1982 Lutheran Episcopal Agreement and the 1983 document Baptism, Eucharist and Ministry, a study produced by the Faith and Order Commission (chaired by Lutheran theologian William Lazareth) of the World Council of Churches. The "Implications of the Gospel" in 1988 began another stage of study and dialogue which led to additional steps by the two churches, known as "Toward Full Communion" and "Concordat of Agreement". [1]

A setback occurred at the ELCA assembly in 1997 when the "Concordat" was voted down, an event which in my mind remains pictured by a tearful face on the front cover of The Lutheran and an inside picture of a dissident whose face was contorted in anger. Two years later the ELCA assembly voted in support of "Called to Common Mission" (CCM), which calls for full communion with the Episcopal Church, and could be implemented on Jan. 1, 2001, if the Episcopal Church votes in approval this year.

The Lutheran approval of CCM last summer has brought a storm of opposition. The dissenters do not agree with the ELCA's acceptance of the historic episcopate, on which the Episcopal Church insists. According to a news release,

> [The dissenters] say it violates Lutheran confessions and threatens Lutheran identity. The historic episcopate is a succession of bishops back to the early Christian Church. As part of CCM, Lutherans would

---

[1] W. Norgren and William G. Rusch (eds.), *"Toward Full Communion" and "Concordat of Agreement"* (Augsburg Fortress, 1991).

install bishops into the historic episcopate, and bishops would perform ordinations. [2]

Those who oppose CCM have recently organized under the name of Word Alone Network and claim that their opposition, especially regarding the historic episcopate, is based on the Lutheran confessions, although some Lutheran churches in other countries are within this tradition. What is back of such strong dissent? Could it possibly come to a schism?

For a moment consider historical background and perspective. Using the Lutheran Book of Worship, on a given Sunday Lutherans throughout our church pray "For the peace of the whole world, for the well-being of the Church of God and for the unity of all," which reflects the high-priestly prayer of Jesus, "That they may all be one". Over the centuries, however, the context has changed, as noted by William Rusch, who was director of the ELCA's Office for Ecumenical Affairs:

> The historical situation we find ourselves in today is vastly different from that of the sixteenth century. The question is no longer that of preserving an existing church unity, but of reestablishing a communion...which has suffered many breaks... In the sixteenth century the catholic church was rent asunder... Today, after centuries of division and mutual condemnation, the church struggles to give the gospel a common voice. Then disunity was an unfortunate and temporary necessity in order to preserve the gospel's integrity; today the achievement of the church's unity is necessary... [3]

An ELCA pastor who is a professor at the Episcopal School of Theology at the University of the South in Sewanee, Tenn., the Rev. Donald Armentrout, stated that "We should adopt the historic episco-pate not for apostolicity but for the sake of catholicity, for the unity of the church. It is the way most of the world's Christians organize themselves". [4]

---

[2] "ELCA Council Sets Implementation Date," ELCA News Service, April 10, 2000.

[3] William G. Rusch, *A Commentary on "Ecumenism: the Vision of the ELCA"* (Augsburg Fortress 1990), p. 33. Rusch was also present at the 1988 meeting held at St. James with Bishops Browning and Chilstrom.

[4] "Wartburg speaker says historic episcopate for unity, not salvation," ELCA News Service, April 7, 2000. The following quotation is from this source.

Lutherans dropped the historic episcopate out of necessity during the sixteenth-century Reformation. When Roman Catholic bishops did not join the Lutheran movement it was necessary for the reformers to drop the practice, despite a desire to maintain it. Armentrout cited "Article 14 of the Apology of the Augsburg Confession, a Lutheran confessional document, in which the reformers affirmed their desire to maintain historical ecclesiastical orders that included ordination by bishops within the historic episcopate". He added that the Episcopal Church and the ELCA "are in agreement in all major issues of faith... CCM is about reconciliation at the level of order and polity. We do this not because [the historic episcopate] is essential for salvation but for the sake of unity in the church".

Another writer, the Rev. Leonard R. Klein, referred to the four marks of the Church as noted in the Nicene Creed, stating that

> An ordered ministry of bishops is no more a gratuitous addition to salvation through Christ alone than is our profession of the Third Article, which commits us to faith in "one, holy, catholic and apostolic Church." Episcopal ordination, taken for granted [by the reformers] at Augsburg, can hardly now be regarded as an alien imposition that ends the freedom of the Gospel. [5]

This brings to mind the tension between the evangelical and catholic sides of Lutheranism. The two terms have often been used with limited understanding. "Evangelical" refers essentially to the Gospel, not to Protestants or Fundamentalists. On the other side, "catholic" does not refer to Rome but to the whole Church in broad scope. Luther the Reformer was evangelical in that he insisted on the open proclamation of the Gospel. But he would also affirm catholicity, affirming "all that is edifying and authentic in the life of the Church of every time and every place," as noted in the *Lutheran Book of Worship* (p. 6).

Opponents of CCM appear to lose their balance in the symbolism of the name they have taken, "Word Alone," according to Klein. He noted that, if they were truly steeped in the Lutheran Confessions, they would have chosen "Word and Sacraments," which is closer to the "living center of Lutheran life". Moreover, he suggested that the opposition may be cultural rather than theological, reflecting anti-clerical or anti-institutional leanings. If one were to press individualism or con-gregationalism too far, there is the danger of losing catholicity and becoming a sect, ever smaller in the search for

---

[5] Leonard R. Klein, "Forum Letter," April 2000. Klein is a former editor of *Lutheran Forum* and is now pastor of Christ Lutheran Church, York, Pa.

Episcopalians and Lutherans 43

doctrinal purity or homogeneity. Saddened by the anger shown by the opponents to CCM, I wrote a letter of support to Bishop H. George Anderson and received a gracious reply, quoted in part:

> Thank you so much for your kind and affirming letter regarding my response in the continuing controversy surrounding the adoption of "Called to Common Mission." As you say, some of the comments voiced in recent months have been harsh and strident. I am encouraged that most of the debate continues within a climate of mutual respect and Christian love. We need to continue encouraging this kind of discussion. I share your conviction that the Augsburg Confession was a conciliatory document. I pray that we find a way to honor the decision of a Churchwide Assembly and also embrace those who continue to dissent.

A concluding thought: In the midst of prima donna pastors (an occupational hazard) one was heard to say that "if there must be oversight, it will be either by bishop or committee—but I prefer bishop".

15

Elian and the Miami Cubans

May 10, 2000

The battle of the Miami Cubans, Cuba, and Washington over the boy Elian is no longer in the headlines but it has brought to mind other battles, often ignored but nonetheless significant. One editorial noted that Elian "became, and remains, a captive of the poisonous relationship between Cuba and the United States. Since 1960, the two countries have neither traded nor had diplomatic relations with each other". [1]

The battle is in diplomatic relationships. The "poisonous relationship" between Cuba and the United States has been kept alive and in the public eye by the Miami Cubans, who have become a strong voting force in Florida and have almost dictated national policy toward Cuba. That power is now being challenged as churches and business groups, such as the U. S. Chamber of Commerce and the Farm Bureau want the embargo to be lifted. Now that the administration as well as the congressional leadership appear to favor improving relations with China, either for business opportunity or as leverage to improve human rights, it is hard to justify the attempt to isolate Cuba, an attempt which is not working anyway.

Another battle has its roots in history but continues to be fought to this day in much of Latin America. From the time of the Spanish conquest to the present there has been a struggle between the "haves" and the "have-nots". On the one hand are the rich landholders, the aristocrats, upper echelon military officers and upper level church leaders. On the other hand are the vast majority of the people, many educators and intellectuals, and many clergy.

It is not necessary to study previous centuries. We need only look back to 1980 when Archbishop Oscar Romero was murdered in El Salvador by the right wing. Before Romero was appointed to that office he was clearly identified with the privileged "haves" but when

---

[1] *The Economist*, April 22, 2000, p. 13. At a meeting of a local stamp club (Oregon Stamp Society) a dealer told me that it was not legal to buy or sell any Cuban stamps issued or in use after 1960, "although it's done all the time".

he became Archbishop he seriously took responsibility for the 90% of the people, the poor and neglected, if not oppressed. His murder took place not on the sidewalk but during the Eucharistic Prayer in the Mass. The murder was intended to be symbolic opposition to the church's newly assumed social concern.

Another example of the simmering (or boiling) conflict is in the southernmost state of Mexico, Chiapas, which has been the scene of a revolution. It has not greatly disrupted Mexican life but it has been a significant embarrassment to the established order. An interesting aspect of the Chiapas story is that we have another example of the Roman Catholic Church moving away from its alliance with power and wealth toward a defense of the common people. With the appeal of liberation theology and the policy statements of Medellín and Puebla, many of the bishops have become sensitive to the needs of the powerless or marginal people.

The hot anger of the Miami Cubans may be seen in the historical context just mentioned. *The Economist* quoted David Rieff, the author of two books about Miami, who called it "an out-of-control banana republic" and offered the following description.

> The Cubans of Miami are America's most successful post-war immigrants... They dominate the politics and economy of southern Florida. Their mean household income...is $50,250, ...more than the average national Latino average... The Cubans who fled in the 1960s were an educated elite, schooled in the tradition that Cuba was the most sophisticated country in Latin America. The Cubans came to America not because they chose to better themselves. They came because a political upheaval drove them. [2]

It has been noted that the hatred Miami Cubans have for Fidel Castro may be explained not in political ideology but simply that Castro took away the privileges of these upper class people, their high incomes, their servants, their good life. There is no need to defend Castro or his excesses, but it must be noted that in spite of austerity and the blockade, Castro has led Cuba to provide basic health care for every Cuban and the virtual elimination of illiteracy. I recall statistics of some years ago in which the infant mortality rate in Cuba was less than in Washington, D.C. The battle of the haves and the have-nots continues.

A third battle might be labeled anti-communism, although another name is now in order. Nevertheless, for much of the century

---

[2] "The Tragedy of Elian," *The Economist*, April 8, 2000, pp. 27-28.

just past the guiding theme for America appeared to be a negativisim, to be against communism. This was a reason given by the Eisenhower administration for entering Guatemala and this was a reason for abetting the assassination of Salvador Allende, the elected president of Chile (and installing a dictator). Also, this was the reason used by Reagan for supporting the Contras in Nicaragua and elsewhere in Central America. [3] This involvement by the United States in Latin America can be traced throughout our history. For example, Calvin Coolidge kept a contingent of Marines in Nicaragua, not under the excuse of anti-communism but to promote U.S. business interests.

Whatever the reasons for involvement, one factor causing historic unrest and instability must certainly be seen in the neglect or oppression of large percentages of the population by a minority composed of the rich and powerful. A current problem is the rise of another excuse for U.S. involvement: the drug war. One political observer wrote:

> In the near term I believe that U.S. foreign policy will be focused, like it or not, on the arc of crisis in Latin America—Colombia, Venezuela and Ecuador... It is Latin America and the Caribbean that most directly affect Americans at home: immigration and drugs fuel the fears of the electorate. What we are seeing now in Colombia...is an American involvement in fighting a guerrilla war under the guise of helping the Colombian army stamp out the drug dealers... The likelihood that U.S. military advisers will be drawn into the struggle is growing, which puts the united States, as in Vietnam, squarely into the counter-insurgency fight. [4]

In each of these battles it is evident that a significant factor is the tension between the few "haves" and the many "have-nots". It is also evident that in parts of Latin America, especially the unstable areas, the middle class is negligible, which suggests a disturbing factor: In the United States we should not take social stability for granted. Robert Reich, a former Secretary of Labor, wrote that

> The average pay of chief executives of major companies rose 18% in 1999, to $12 million. (Back in 1990, it was a modest $1.8 million.) ...

---

[3] It has been noted that after expelling Somoza (who fled to Miami), there were 14 ex-priests at cabinet level in the new government of Nicaragua. Prior to that time it was my privilege to meet one of these priests at a conference center (CIDOC) in Cuernavaca, Mexico.

[4] James Chace, "The Next New Threat," *World Policy Journal* XVII:1 (Spring 2000), pp. 113-115. Chace is editor of the journal.

Now switch your sights to the 400 janitors who recently blocked traffic in Los Angeles... They earn $6.80 to $7.90 per hour... The median wage of child care workers is $6.60 an hour, usually without benefits... This year the richest 2.7 million Americans, comprising the top 1 percent, will have as many after-tax dollars to spend as the bottom 100 million put together. [5]

Is a trend discernible?

The story of Elian triggered the thoughts of these battles (areas of conflict) but consideration of our country's involvement in Latin America, some of it for good and some not so good, brings to mind this saying: "Ah, poor Mexico, poor Mexico, so far from God... and so close to the United States". A bit of self-criticism can be healthy.

---

[5] Robert Reich, "The Great Divide," *The American Prospect* (May 8, 2000), p. 56.

16

Postage Stamps Reflect Society

July 15, 2000

Although it has not been a shock, I have come to the realization that at my age I have lived through numerous events which may be considered ancient history by the younger generation or may be studied as factors within complex trends. In younger years I dealt with the issues at hand, preoccupied with the struggle to survive and unable to see the large picture. More reflective now, though not from a rocking chair, I have been eager to collect the series of "Celebrate the Century" postage stamps. For each decade of the century just ended the U.S. Postal Service issued one pane with 15 stamps depicting key images of the decade. [1] Imagine selecting 15 pictures with which to characterize ten years. What a difficult task it is to see the big picture. True objectivity is next to impossible because, among other things, each of us has a distinct perspective, an attitude which shapes a particular view of the world. [2]

One stamp for the decade of the 1920s, titled "The Gatsby Style," led me to the background pages which had references to various authors who attempted to describe the "hedonistic world of the idle rich". Describing the "flappers of the naughty and exuberant '20s," the background page noted that the "nation was flush [and] money and booze were everywhere". But all this came to an end suddenly with the stock market crash.

Moving on to the 1930s, a stamp depicting the Depression was the picture of a tired woman with a hopeless expression and two children leaning against her. The descriptive pages had a picture of a shantytown and a Will Rogers' quotation: "The working classes didn't bring this on, it was the big boys that thought the financial drunk

---

[1] In addition to a brief description printed on the back of each stamp, the Postal Service issued a volume for each decade describing the 15 stamps chosen for the decade. The ten volumes of *Celebrate the Century* with many photos and simple text are in the Central Library.

[2] I should ask Pastor Manicke about the meaning of the German word "Weltanschauung."

was going to last forever". Also pictured was a bread line with a sign requesting donations to feed the hungry.

This Depression image jolted my thoughts to current realities. Why do I not like to face the panhandlers on the street, even now when I do not always wear a clerical collar? How would I have dealt with the obvious and widespread needs of the 1930s? Because many of us have been reared with the understanding of the twin commands to love God and love neighbor as well as the parable of the Good Samaritan, it is difficult to meet a beggar, who may or may not have true needs. Occasionally when there is a television presentation of someone in acute need there is an outpouring of support. That's great but what about the countless others whose pictures do not appear on the screen?

Humanitarian action is an individual's worthy response to need. However, to praise individual action while neglecting the large structures of society is unconscionable. By combining the offerings of many individuals, as in the Hunger Fund of the ELCA, much can be accomplished around the globe. In the 1980s the president suggested that taxes could be reduced by turning responsibility for humanitarian aid over to the churches. What a boon for those who give no church offerings and it might also absolve consciences. However, the good will of all the churches together could not solve numerous complex problems.

Consider the health needs of 35 to 40 million Americans who are without health insurance. The World Health Organization recently announced the results of a survey of the health care systems in 191 nations, finding that the United States ranked 37th.

> The U.S. health care system is inferior to those of most other industrialized nations because it is the most expensive and yet fails to provide adequate care to the poor... The top 10 percent here are the healthiest in the world... It's the bottom five or 10 percent [with] health conditions as bad as those in sub-Saharan Africa... "Given that the U.S. outspends everybody by such a degree, the conclusion is that (the health care system) is very inefficient"... The United States also is poor at the low-cost preventive care that keeps Europeans healthy. [3]

France and Italy are at the top of the listing along with all of industrialized Europe. Consider also other problems, such as the tremendous inequalities of income and the trend which makes the

---

[3] "Survey faults U.S. health care system," *The Oregonian,* June 21, 2000.

gap between rich and poor ever greater. Moreover, consider the demands of the rich countries for resources and labor in the poor countries, often with destabilizing results.

It is obvious that political, economic and social complexities are beyond the reach of humanitarian acts on an individual basis. Clearly involved in humanitarianism is a network of government, the United Nations, and what are called non-governmental organizations (NGOs). In spite of some setbacks, as in Somalia and the former Yugoslavia, we like to assume that there are basic principles and public attitudes on which humanitarian assistance is based. Thus, it was a surprise for me to read the opinion of a political scientist, William DeMars, as follows:

> In the modern history of humanitarian action dating from civilian relief during the Second World War, never before has the legitimacy of the enterprise been so profoundly and publicly challenged, while at the same time never have the services of humanitarian organizations been more in demand. [4]

One reason for the "crisis of conscience" in humanitarian aid, he claimed, has been the changing nature of warfare, particularly in Africa. He stated that "the strategies of internal conflict have shifted from military coup in the 1960s to protracted war in the 1970s and 1980s, to warlordism in the 1990s". Concluding that human suffering will increase, he added that "war without mercy can hardly be regarded as progressive". Whether in Africa or here in the United States, humanitarian concern is a worthy attitude for an individual but government is a necessary partner in facing almost overwhelming needs. Lutheran theologian Martin E. Marty wrote:

> A nation cannot long endure a climate in which individuals prosper and the common good turns uncommonly bad. All enterprise depends upon a foundation in a civil society, which always needs tending... The reality of greed culture will finally meet its match in the realization of a more civil society. [5]

---

[4] William DeMars, "War and Mercy in Africa," *World Policy Journal* XVII:2 (Summer 2000), pp. 1-10. DeMars has taught international relations at the American University in Cairo and at Notre Dame.

[5] Martin E. Marty, "'Civil society' is at risk from a culture of greed," *The Oregonian*, May 6, 2000. Marty is a professor emeritus at the University of Chicago.

Florence Nightingale and Clara Maass

August 14, 2000

Religion is back in the news with Al Gore's selection of an Orthodox Jew as his choice for a running mate. Political columnists have written about Joseph Lieberman's integrity, noting that his political record reflects his faith. One newswriter stated that in Orthodox Judaism there is "a fundamental belief in one God and in God's role in the world. From the first thing in the morning until the last moments before sleep, an observant Jew constantly acknowledges–and is reminded–of God's presence". [1]

This attention to religion in the political news is a welcome turn from the strong influence of the right wing in religion, which at times appears to claim an exclusive use of the word "Christian". In this right wing there is a ready formula to "accept Jesus Christ as your personal Lord and Savior". Once this formula is stated, ethics frequently amounts to a hard line statement of individualistic "do nots," reflecting the movement's absolute conviction that they are right–and they want a government which will enforce their correct views. How strange that the religious rightists would support Reagan who did not identify with any church but simply stated "the formula" whereas Carter, who continually expressed his faith, was rejected.

Two remarkable examples of persons who gave their lives as expressions of faith were remembered this past Sunday, August 13, which was a day of commemoration for Florence Nightingale and Clara Maass, pioneers in the field of nursing. [2] First, the example of Florence Nightingale. Her parents were well to do and she grew up in the family homes in London and in the country. But she found the customary social life to be unsatisfying and began studying public health and hospitals, subjects ignored by most people at the time. A friend sent her a Yearbook of the Kaiserwerth (Germany) Motherhouse of Deaconesses and in 1850 (mid century) she enrolled for training as

---

[1] Sara Rubenstein, "Balance between God and work," *The Oregonian*, Aug. 13, 2000.

[2] "Days of Commemoration," *Lutheran Book of Worship*, p. 11.

a nurse. Here, incidentally, was a Lutheran influence, an institution organized by Pastor Theodor Fliedner to train sisters who would serve in nursing, education or the care of the old. Through the influence of Pastor Fliedner there were soon deaconesses in England, America, and elsewhere.

Having completed her training, Florence Nightingale found herself in 1854 leading a party of nurses to Turkey to care for British soldiers wounded in the Crimean War. They found conditions intolerable and the doctors of that age were hostile to the nurses (or to their new ideas in care). But her passion for aiding the wounded won her reputation as a heroic figure. Later in England, once again under strong opposition, she worked for the reform of workhouses. Her tombstone reads simply: "F. N. Born 1820. Died 1910." [3]

A second example is Clara Maass, the daughter of German immigrant parents in New Jersey, she was one of the first five graduates of a Lutheran nursing school. Before the Army Nurse Corps had been established, she served in the army on a contract basis during the Spanish American War in 1898-99. At a camp in Santiago, Cuba, she was introduced to the horrors of yellow fever. [4] Her next tour of duty took her to the Philippines, where again she nursed the victims of yellow fever. There she contracted another fever (bonebreak fever) and was sent home.

Meanwhile a Cuba-U.S. research project in Havana had singled out the mosquito as the probable transmitter of yellow fever. According to author Pfatteicher, quoted above:

> Clara Maass was one of twenty people who responded to the call for subjects in experimentation. Her first mosquito bite led to a slight case of yellow fever from which she soon recovered, but ten days after she was bitten a second time she died. She was the only woman and the only American to give her life in the research... Yellow fever [thanks to this research] is now preventable.

Thus Clara Maass offered herself for the role of a non-vaccinated human guinea pig and, contracting the disease, she died, but she

---

[3] Philip H. Pfatteicher "Aug. 13, Florence Nightingale, Clara Maass," *Festivals and Commemorations*, Augsburg, 1980, pp. 320-324.

[4] Incidentally, years ago I had occasion to make a brief stop in Santiago, Cuba, while en route to Havana but at the time I did not know about the town's association with Clara Maass. Teddy Roosevelt's adventures at San Juan Hill, near Santiago, are well known.

helped wipe out yellow fever. Eventually, after a year, the army returned her body to New Jersey for the family to bury. Soon her grave was forgotten.

However, there is more to the story, as I discovered from a letter written (Jan. 22, 1954) by my father following visits to some congregations in Virginia. One of the pastors told him about a parishioner whom he and the congregation were helping. She was Leopolda Gynther, R.N., who was spending her retirement years in a one-woman campaign, determined to obtain recognition from the U.S. and Cuban governments for Clara and to build a suitable memorial over Clara's grave. According to the letter, my father spoke to Ms. Gynther by telephone and learned that she had made six trips to Havana, found some witnesses and searched records in Havana and Washington. He wrote that as a result of Gynther's work the "Cuban government celebrated a Clara Maass Day and issued a Clara Maass postage stamp. The U. S. also issued a [beautiful] postage stamp". And in 1952 the hospital where she trained changed its name to the Clara Maass Memorial Hospital.

The lives of Florence Nightingale and Clara Maass reflected God's living presence. Thus it is refreshing to read in the political news of this aspect of religion, as noted that Lieberman holds a faith which "constantly acknowledges–and is reminded of–God's presence". [5] This is in contrast to the right wing's uncomfortable absolutism, a certainty about everything which, according to columnist Anthony Lewis, "has been the hallmark of totalitarian movements". Religionists on the right use the Bible as a rule book, a book of statutes or a code for living, often being quite selective in the verses chosen for the authoritative "don'ts".

Lutherans should appreciate the distinctive understanding of the Word of God, not simply as the written Word, the printed pages of the Bible, but also as the living Word, the person Jesus Christ. The reference at the opening of John's Gospel clearly shows that God's Word is not limited to print: "In the beginning was the Word, and the Word was with God, and the Word was God. He [the Word] was in the beginning with God". This is made exceptionally clear in verse 14, "And the Word became flesh and lived among us, and we have seen his glory, the glory of the father's only son".

---

[5] *New York Times'* interviews on religion with presidential candidates Bush and Gore are reported in Molly Ivins, *Shrub: The Short and Happy Political Life of George W. Bush* (Random House, 2000), pp. 57-60. The contrast in these interviews is vivid.

18

Christians: In Community or Loners

August 30, 2000

While reading a magazine a particular title caught my attention: "The Social Recession". It was the title to a section of book reviews in which the author, George Scialabra, reviewed several books, whose titles also called for attention. [1] One of the books was *The American Paradox: Spiritual Hunger in an Age of Plenty* by David Myers; another was *The Loss of Happiness in Market Democracies* by Robert E. Lane.

The point was made that in our developed countries more people are rich than ever before (aside from the extremes of wealth and poverty) but also more people are unhappy. Apparently the reasons for unhappiness in the past, simply stated, were "constraints" from ethics, laws or social custom and "scarcity," presumably of goods. The modern age, however, has brought changes in the causes of unhappiness, an idea which has been studied by well known sociologists and historians. [2] The author stated that "the way we live has its costs," adding that

> The awkward truth appears to be that constraints are also supports, choices are also stresses, and breadth of experience may sometimes be the enemy of depth.

Crediting Myers with the term "social recession," he stated that there is considerable data on the subject. As an example he referred to the marriage crisis, noting that since 1960 "co-habitation is seven times more frequent," "four out of ten ninth-graders report having had sexual intercourse," "births to unmarried teens have quadrupled,"

---

[1] George Scialabra, "The Social Recession," *The American Prospect*, Sept. 11, 2000, pp. 50-52. The books reviewed were published by Yale University Press.

[2] The author mentioned Émile Durkheim, Max Weber, Robert Putnam and Francis Fukuyama (*Great Disruption*).

and "forty percent of all children do not live with their biological fathers".

The authors of both books reviewed agreed that poverty is not the prime cause of the social recession. They (Myers and Lane) were both sharply critical of the economic inequality in this country but their books were "less concerned with injustice or exploitation than with individualism and its unintended consequences".

Referring again to the obvious example of marital instability, Myers noted that there are many causes beyond individual considerations, such as the disappearance of neighborhoods, the changing nature of work, economic progress of women, the declining efficacy of religious sanctions and sexualization of advertising. Individualism is not seen as evil but in broad concepts it is a factor in a social recession. The book reviewer noted Lane's description of some

> Sources of happiness ("intrinsic work enjoyment, family solidarity, social inclusion, sociability at the workplace") and unhappiness (chronic financial insecurity, overwork, etc.), [which have led to these consequences:] "There is a kind of famine of warm interpersonal relations, of easy-to-reach neighbors, or encircling inclusive memberships, and of solidarity family life… For people lacking in social support of this kind, unemployment has more serious effects, illnesses are more deadly, disappointment with one's children is harder to bear, bouts of depression last longer, and frustration and failed expectation of all kinds are more traumatic."

In the conclusion of this section of book reviews, the author stated "Let's hope for a prophet," adding that with the "multitude of opposing voices," the market, television, advertising and the Internet, "all ceaselessly shrilling our little desires in our ears, it's hard to be optimistic".

On the other hand, there *are* prophets and teachers. If a major cause of the social recession is "individualism and its unintended consequences," there are those who are addressing the subject. Martha Ellen Stortz, a professor at Pacific Lutheran Theological Seminary, has written about the

> Legacy of individualism that…fashions people as solitary moral agents and makes moral debate a matter of conflicting opinions: my ethics versus your ethics… [Thus:] Moral deliberation, discernment, and formation lose any input from a community… Luther is deeply aware of how relationships constitute both the individual and the community. His explanation of the Fourth Commandment creates a

taxonomy of reciprocal relationships between parents and children, church and believers, citizen and state. [3]

Many Christians have given individualistic interpretations to St. Paul's writings on ethics. For example, Philippians 1:27 states "Live your life in a manner worthy of the gospel of Christ" and another translation (King James) reads "Let your conversation be as it becometh the gospel…" David Fredrickson, a Bible scholar, has written that St. Paul is encouraging his readers to "engage actively through speech in the affairs of their own assembly," suggesting that the reference applies to the political process. [4] Earlier in the same chapter, in verses 9-11 there is the understanding that the community interacts for the common good, as though there is a testing in the community's search for consensus.

Surely we are not created to be hermits; neither are we intended to be "loner Christians". A starting point could well be the congregation, for we are baptized into the community, a community of moral deliberation. A study entitled "Living in Communion," sponsored by the Lutheran World Federation, speaks of a challenge for the churches, in which it is noted that "Communion means sharing, giving and taking, cooperation, exchange, joint participation, interaction". [5] These words can be applied to a consideration of the excesses of individualism. However, the same concept can apply in ever widening circles reaching through the political process to the city, the nation, and the nations of the world.

During a social recession the Christian is not restricted to self-centered individualism but is an individual living in communion and reflecting the light of Christ.

---

[3] Martha Ellen Stortz, "Practicing Christians" in *The Promise of Lutheran Ethics*, edited by Karen L. Bloomquist and John R. Stumme (Fortress Press, 1998), 60-61.

[4] David Fredrickson, "Pauline Ethics" in *The Promise of Lutheran Ethics*," Bloomquist and Stumme (eds.), 120.

[5] *Living in Communion*, LWF Studies No. 35 (Lutheran World Federation, Geneva), p. 98.

19

Palestinian Land

November 5, 2000

Boys throwing stones, suicide bombers, exchanges of gunfire, police in armored vehicles, bulldozers tearing down houses, faces contorted in anger—these are the pictures in the news of the clash between Jews and Palestinians in the Middle East. One can only imagine the ingrained hatred which could almost take genetic proportions. And one can wonder about the causes of this conflict.

Prompted to review an article on this subject which I wrote more than 20 years ago, it is clear that the argument continues to be valid.

> Justification for the establishment of the state of Israel in Palestine has been argued on the basis of many claims—political, biblical or historical. However, since there is no common yardstick of measurement and since each claim has a counter-claim, it is likely that there will be no generally acceptable justification for the Zionist's cause. [1]

Of the three claims, consider first the political claim of Zionism to Palestinian land. The establishment of the political state of Israel in 1948 was the fulfillment of a Zionist dream, expressed by Theodor Herzl, a Hungarian-born journalist in 1896 and a year later at a Zionist Congress in Basel, Switzerland. For various reasons emotions were high in a dream for a national state, though not necessarily in Palestine. Jews faced anti-Semitic legislation in the late nineteenth century and during the 1880s hundreds were killed in Poland and White Russia. Moreover, the ideals of the French Revolution encouraged nationalist movements in Europe. In 1917 the British Foreign Secretary, Lord Balfour made an equivocal statement, which was generally interpreted as support for the establishment of a Jewish state in Palestine: "His Majesty's Government view with favor the establishment in Palestine

---

[1] William C. Arbaugh, "Israel's Claim for Palestinian Land," *University of Portland Review*, XXIX:2 (Fall 1977), pp. 5-14 —on which this issue of "Musings" is based.

of a national home for the Jewish people..." However, the remainder of the sentence was generally ignored: "it being clearly understood that nothing shall be done which may prejudice the civil and religious rights of existing non-Jewish communities in Palestine". Strong factors in public opinion at a later date were revelations of atrocities of the holocaust, the displacement of many people and the shifting of various national boundaries following World War II in 1945.

The problem of self-determination has not been eased by the rapid rise of the Jewish population in the land. According to estimates made by the United Nations, in 1914 the Jews in Palestine numbered 6 or 7% of the population, changing to 650,000 or about 33% of the population by 1946, two years before the creation of the state of Israel—an alarming change for the Arabs. To this can be added the plight of Palestinian refugees, who refuse to be resettled, not wanting to relinquish their rights to their old properties in what is now Israel.

In the second place there is a biblical basis to Israel's claim to Palestine, the land of God's promise to Abraham. According to the Old Testament book of Genesis, God commanded Abram to go to a new land, promising to give him the land, to make a great nation, and through him to offer blessing for all people (Genesis 12:3). The problem with this religious claim is not its validity to the Jew, but the lack of an acceptable interpretation from other religious views. Christians and Muslims also recognize the Patriarch Abraham and the covenant. Muslims claim their descent from Abraham and his son by Hagar, Ishamael. Although the Jews claimed continuity of the covenant blessing, the descendants of Ishamael were not without God's blessing (Gen. 17:20). Christians also recognize the validity of the Old Testament covenant, but they look at it from the perspective of the New Testament, that God established a new covenant in Jesus Christ, fulfilling the promise that "all families of the earth would be blessed". The blessing is in Jesus Christ.

Palestine is a holy place to the Jews because of rich associations with their covenant history but Palestine and Jerusalem are also holy to the Christians for many well-known reasons. Moreover, these are also holy places for Muslims. Abraham, their progenitor is buried there and it was from the Dome of the Rock, covering Rock Moriah, that Mohammed is said to have ascended to heaven.

A third argument by which Israel has claimed the land of Palestine is the historical claim. Although the land has been claimed from the time of Abraham, actual control of the land was neither extensive in time nor continuous. Palestine for ages has been a crossroads for the surrounding nations. Since the patriarchal age of Abraham in the twentieth or nineteenth century B.C. ancient Canaanites were subject to rulers from Egyptian, Hyksos, and Hittite powers in succeeding waves. Following the exodus from Egypt, the Jews did not actually control Palestine until the days of David and Solomon from 1000 to 927 B.C. After the death of Solomon the kingdom fell apart, dividing into two. The northern kingdom, Israel, in spite of alliances with Syria, fell to the Assyrians in 722 B.C. Judah, the southern kingdom, did survive until Nebuchadnezzar of Babylon destroyed Jerusalem in 586 B.C. and marched the Judeans into captivity. But in 538 B.C. the Persians conquered the Babylonians and allowed some of the captive Jews to return to Jerusalem.

Other conquerors appeared and disappeared. Alexander the Great conquered an empire for the Greeks, including Palestine in 330 B.C. When the empire was weakened Palestinian Jews under Simon Maccabaeus and John Hyrcanus revolted, claiming an independence which lasted 72 years. Then came Roman rule until A.D. 638 when Arab followers of Mohammed took control of the Middle East, raced across North Africa and into Europe. However, not all Muslims were Arabs. The Ottoman Turks had control of Palestine for about 400 years prior to World War I when Palestine became a British mandate.[2]

Because the claims for this land cannot be justified in a manner acceptable to the contending parties, moderation should be encouraged. But is moderation possible given the political realities?[3] Whether realistic or not, might a case be made for United Nations control?

---

[2] The length of rule in years by various conquerors has been summarized: Egypt 615, Jews 414, Romans 677, Arabs 447, Turkey 601, according to Ilene Beatty, *Arab and Jew in the Land of Canaan* (Henry Regnery Co. 1957), p. 49.

[3] SEARCH is an ecumenical organization which "believes that justice for Palestinians and security for Israeli Jews are not mutually exclusive but interdependent". Supporters include several Lutheran bishops, including retired ELCA Bp. Chilstrom. SEARCH for Justice and Equality in Palestine/Israel, P.O. Box 3452, Framingham, MA 01705-3452.

A Christmas Carol

December 18, 2000

Christmas carols are delightful. The Messiah's birth, anticipated with eager longing over the centuries, must necessarily be an emotional high point, as in "Come, thou long-expected Jesus, Born to set thy people free". Emotional pressure is also evident outside of the faith among those who are philosophizing sentiment, as in "Yes, Virginia, there is a Santa Claus". Non-believers also recognize the benefits of sentimental carols in softening the hearts of consumers as they wander the shopping malls.

The carols of Christmas have sometimes been written in the heat of ideological battle, reflecting controversy. Christmas itself has often been in the crossfire of religion and government. There was nothing fuzzy or sentimental about Herod's reaction to the birth of Jesus. Herod acted decisively. On the other hand, much can be said about governmental support of religion, frequently given with a heavy hand. Strangely, some Protestants have used the power of government to suppress the celebration of Christmas, as in Scotland and New England. In our current multi-cultural and multi-faith America the debate regarding a creche in the public square appears superficial. Let the malls (who know what's good for business) build the public creche while Christians instead battle to provide answers to unmet social needs.

"Of the Father's love begotten" (LBW 42), one of my favorite Christmas carols, was not written as a carol but as a defense of the faith. The author, Marcus Aurelius Clemens Prudentius (348-413), was fighting for his faith in the midst of a serious struggle. It was not long before he was born that Christianity had been given legal rights. Nonetheless, an opposition remained from the time it was an outlaw religion.

Born in Zaragoza, Spain, Prudentius studied law and twice served as a magistrate. Respected as a judge, Prudentius was called to Rome by Emperor Theodosius to serve in his court. Among other things Prudentius attempted to stop or restrict the gladiatorial shows. At the height of his career he made an abrupt change.

> At age fifty-seven, convinced of the vanity and impermanence of most of life, he retired to a life of poverty and seclusion, and began to write the works which were so widely read and influential during the Middle Ages, and from which many fine Christian hymns have been drawn. [1]

The battleground was theological. For a couple centuries there were heated debates regarding the nature of Christ and the Trinity. Was Christ truly God or a demi-god, a half-way step? Was Jesus Christ simply a human being, a created being or was he truly God? Against serious attacks the Church responded with the Nicene Creed, using impressive vocabulary and phrasing to state the fundamental beliefs, as in the following:

> We believe in one Lord, Jesus Christ, the only Son of God, eternally begotten of the Father, God from God, Light from Light, true God from true God, begotten, not made, of one Being with the Father. Through him [Christ] all things were made. For us and for our salvation he came down from heaven.

In this context we see the opening lines of the carol by Prudentius, emphasizing that Christ was not a created being. He did not begin his life when he was born in Bethlehem. He lived before—always—with God, as God. How could God be created? He always was before the planets were whirling, "Ere the worlds began to be". Thus:

> Of the Father's love begotten / Ere the worlds began to be, / He is Alpha and Omega, He the source, the ending he, / Of the things that are, that have been, and that future years shall see, / Evermore and evermore.

This thought is expressed in the opening of John's Gospel, in which Christ is described as the living Word:

> In the beginning was the Word, and the Word was with God, and the Word was God. He was in the beginning with God. All things came into being through him [the Word]...

---

[1] Marilyn Kay Stulken, *Hymnal Companion to the Lutheran Book of Worship* (Fortress Press, 1981), pp. 142-143. In addition to "Of the Father's love begotten" (42), the *Lutheran Book of Worship* also includes "O chief of cities, Bethlehem" (81) by Prudentius.

> What has come into being in him was life, and the life was the light of all people... And the Word became flesh and lived among us, and we have seen his glory, the glory as of a father's only son, full of grace and truth [John 1:1-4, 14].

Here is the mystery of the person of Christ, the word incarnate (in the flesh). A word is a form of communication and God is communicating with us not alone with a "written Word" but with the "living Word". It has been said that in this reading from John we have the theoretical view of Luke's Christmas account.

The promise given to Abraham at the beginning of his journey in faith, that "in you all the families of the earth shall be blessed," is fulfilled in this "birth forever blessed". [2] As Prudentius noted,

> This is he whom seers in old time / Chanted of with one accord, / Whom the voices of the prophets / Promised in their faithful word; / Now he shines, the long expected; / Let creation praise its Lord / Evermore and evermore.

Ideological battles have been fought on many a turf. Prudentius made use of his writing, influential centuries after his death. We also should recognize the need to express our faith beyond the gratification of sentiment. The Herods of this world should not be the only realists or activists. Christians need to fight the battle of faith on many fronts (including the political) and join Prudentius in singing

> Christ, to thee, with God the Father, / And, O Holy Ghost, to thee, / Hymn and chant and high thanksgiving / And unwearied praises be: / Honor, glory, and dominion, / And eternal victory / Evermore and evermore! Amen.

---

[2] Gen. 12:3; the carol by Prudentius.

21

Quo Vadis?

January 3, 2001

One summer it was my privilege to spend some time in seminar groups at a conference center in Cuernavaca, Mexico.[1] While there I enjoyed reading the names on various storefronts and businesses, some of which revealed creative imagination. For example, one enterprising venture had the Latin name "Quo Vadis," which means "Where are you going?" The establishment so named was a mortuary.

It's a good question, cutting through peripherals to substance. With the beginning of a new year many of us will be taking stock and making resolutions on a personal basis but the question "Quo vadis?" is also valid for the nation in a global context. It has often been said that for much of the twentieth century the United States has had a negative purpose, understanding itself by what it was against—communism—but not what it was for. Clearly America won the Cold War but America is often now perceived in other countries as being in decline.

Samuel Berger, the Assistant to the President for National Security, has written that in this global age the challenge is to recognize the difference between power and authority.

> Power is the ability to compel by force and sanctions... Authority is the ability to lead... Our authority is built on qualities very different from our power: on the attractiveness of our values, on the force of our example, on the credibility of our commitments, and on our willingness to listen to and stand by others. There may be no real threat to our power today. But if we use *power in a way that antagonizes*

---

[1] The Center for Intercultural Documentation, usually called CIDOC (same acronym in Spanish and pronounced see-dok) was a conference center founded by Ivan Illich, an author and a social critic. Before obtaining laicization he was an assistant to Cardinal Spellman and as a monsignor he organized a study program for priests who would serve in Latin America. He called it a "deyankeefication school".

our friends and dishonors our commitments, we will lose our authority and our power will mean very little. [2]

Regarding our national directions, did the recent elections clarify matters? Apparently not. Over the last couple months there have been some disturbing observations. One columnist, Jane Eisner, quoted Barbara D. Whitehead of Rutgers as follows:

> We missed an opportunity [in the political campaign] to talk broadly about who we are as a people, where we're going, what we should aspire to... How do we care for our children? How can we move toward racial reconciliation? How can we create a more moral culture? ... Are we so wrapped up in our postmodern cocoon, that we view national goals as an intrusion, inspiration as an unnecessary bother? A person's character can evolve over time, so can a nation's. We can summon our more magnanimous impulses and reverse this descent into Me-ism. [3]

Eisner also wrote that Robert Bellah, a professor from the University of California, "has spent a career cataloguing this 'radical individualism' in the American character. This race, he says, "has turned into a consumerist bidding war". One comment on "America's very un-American economic face" stated bluntly that "Unlike Europe, the U.S. is now the land of inequality". [4]

Turning to the global context, it should be embarrassing to us that a private citizen (Ted Turner) offers to pay $34 million toward arrears in U.S. dues to the United Nations, a debt which Congress has refused to fund. This country, the richest and the most powerful, has been seen as whining in its attempt to reduce its obligations to the United Nations. Finally, on Christmas Eve the General Assembly of the U.N. approved a budget reform package which reduces the U.S. share, causing the shortfall to be picked up by 18 developing nations. [5] In this global age is the United States turning isolationist? Is "me-ism" becoming a national trait?

---

[2] Samuel R. Berger, "A Foreign Policy for the Global Age," *Foreign Affairs,* 79:6 (November/December 2000), p. 39.

[3] Jane Eisner, (*The Philadelphia Enquirer*), *The Oregonian,* Nov. 3, 2000.

[4] Geneva Oberholser (Washington Post Writers Group), *The Oregonian,* Nov. 1, 2000.

[5] Edith Lederer (Associated Press), "U.N. Budget overhauled, cutting U.S. payments," *The Oregonian,* Dec. 24, 2000.

Quo Vadis?

Among some broad outlines in foreign policy which Samuel Berger has highlighted is the point that "the disproportionate power America enjoys today is more likely to be accepted by other nations if we use it for something more than self-protection". [6] Noting that the global economy is working in our interest, it also "accentuates the need to alleviate economic disparities". Emphasizing the difference between power and authority, Berger wrote that

> America cannot be a first-rate power on a third-class budget. We should not have to struggle to fund patently vital programs like our effort to secure nuclear materials in Russia... This damages our ability to lead. It is hard to explain to the Japanese, for example, why we can't fund our $35 million share to help denuclearize North Korea (to which they [the Japanese] have contributed $1 billion) when they read of our $2 trillion surplus.
>
> [Berger added] What threatens to alienate our allies today is not that we are wealthy and powerful, but that despite our wealth and power we do not meet our obligations to the U.N. or fully fund our commitment to the development banks, or devote as much of our GDP to the reduction of global poverty as do 16 countries not as wealth...or ratify treaties we urge others to adopt.

The last president of the Soviet Union, Mikhail Gorbachev wrote that "Globalization is a given—but 'American globalization' would be a mistake". He added:

> I would go even further and say it is time for America's electorate to be told the blunt truth: The present situation of the United States, by which a part of its population is able to enjoy a life of extraordinary comfort and privilege, is not tenable over the long run as long as an enormous portion of the world lives in abject poverty, degradation and backwardness. For 10 years, U.S. foreign policy has been formulated as if it were the policy of a victor in war... In fact, there has been no 'pacification'. On the contrary, there has been a heightening of inequalities, tension and hostility, with most of the last directed toward the United States. [7]

Are we able to take criticism? Facing a sign above a mortuary, we should ask ourselves quo vadis?

---

[6] Berger, "A Foreign Policy for the Global Age," pp. 22-39.

[7] Mikhail Gorbachev, "Foreign policy problems will dog new president," *The Oregonian,* Dec. 27, 2000.

22

Lessons From Another Colossus

February 28, 2001

Thumbing through a journal just received, I spotted some comments about black suits, which I happen to favor, and was so intrigued that shortly thereafter I sat down to red the article. The author, historian and editor Karl E. Meyer, was describing the British Empire in the time of Edward VII, noting the sweeping effect of Britain's cultural legacy:

> Beyond money and battleships, imperial Britain deployed a subtler source of universal influence: a culture in the broad sense that admiring and often baffled foreigners strove to imitate... as in the somber fashion of dark suits favored by statesmen, hotel waiters, orchestra conductors, undertakers... [and some clergy]. Interestingly, even Bolsheviks like Lenin, Fascists like Mussolini, and Japanese envoys representing the world's oldest throne, all dressed on state occasions in British black. How else to be taken seriously? [1]

Without pausing to wonder about the cultural influence America has on the world, as with levis and loud music, I could not escape some worrisome parallels as the author described Britain during the Edwardian age, noting

> How a global colossus can be weakened from within by unbridled party rivalry, feeding on outrage over broken rules and dirty tricks, and how swiftly the appearance of permanent supremacy can give way to the reality of diminished authority... With hindsight, this imperial unraveling owed as much to internal dissonance as it did to foreign challenges, and its onset—the first rips in the fabric— occurred during a period erroneously equated with prosperous placidity: the Edwardian era. So bitter were political disputes over trade and taxes, so divisive were class, gender, and ethnic conflicts,

---

[1] Karl E. Meyer, "An Edwardian Warning: The unraveling of a Colossus," *World Policy Journal*, Winter, 2000-2001, pp. 47-57. Meyer is the editor of *World Policy Journal*. Edward VII ruled the British Empire from 1901 to 1910, following the death of Queen Victoria.

that many Britons turned almost with relief to the hecatomb of 1914-18, whose casualties wrote finis to the old imperial swagger.

Although an understanding of history is necessary for perspective, there is a risk in leaping across centuries with sweeping generalities. [2] Nevertheless, this reading reminded me of another article, this one written by Kevin Phillips. [3] What caught my attention was a string of nine pictures arranged in three sets of three: from Britain: King Charles I, Oliver Cromwell, King Charles II; from France: King Louis SVI, Napoleon, King Louis XVIII; and from the U.S.: George H. W. Bush, Bill Clinton, George W. Bush.

Intrigued by these far-reaching analogies, I read on, wondering what the author meant by restorations as he moved across several centuries and several nations. He wrote that

> Restorations in the England of the Stuarts and the France of Bourbons involved the following sequence: The ruling house became extremely unpopular and was dethroned (Charles I in 1649, Louis XVI in 1793). But the revolutionary forces and successful interlopers—Oliver Cromwell and Napoleon—soon became even more unpopular, hated by the displaced power structure and referred to as "the monster". After years of preparation, the gathering forces of the old ruling house found the public forgetful enough of old disdains to permit a tenuous restoration of the old family (Charles II in 1660 and Louis SVIII in 1814).

From this background the author held that George W's election represents a restoration, that is, the return of a ruling family to the position from which it was removed. Phillips held that "the Stuart and Bourbon restorations didn't work out (both houses were chased out again)...because restoration is one of the purest forms of reaction". Further, he wrote that "in the typical restoration, minimally talented family members form a sandwich of mediocrity around a flawed but greater talent". It was unexpectedly strange to see Bill Clinton placed in the company of Cromwell and Napoleon until the author explained his "sandwich" comparisons.

---

[2] At the beginning of his article Meyer recognized a risk in drawing historical parallels: "All historical analogies are a form of sleight of hand, in which the clever conjuror by adroit selection can find points of parallel with almost anything past" (p. 47).

[3] "His Fraudulency the Second?" *The American Prospect,* Jan. 29, 2001, pp. 22-25. Phillips is the author of *The Emerging Republican Majority* and *The Politics of Rich and Poor.*

Does the church have anything to say regarding public or national issues? Can it speak with moral authority? Many religious people, certainly those who now speak loudly, appear to view ethics as individualized matters, not a public ethics. For example, the national treasury expects to be overflowing but has there been any discussion of providing health insurance for those outside the system? Is there a serious desire to strengthen our schools? Obviously lacking is a national vision. In this regard professor Karen Bloomquist wrote:

> Rather than moral consensus drawing people together for the sake of concerted address of injustices, moral fragmentation and an anxious obsession with private ("I want mine!") to exclusion of public concerns now constitutes the prevailing ethos. [4]

Continuing the risky venture of broad generalizations and leapfrogging generations, historian Meyer in the article quoted above noted that when Winston Churchill wrote about the problems leading to World war I, he dated the beginning of "these violent times" with the complacency, prosperity and infighting of the Edwardian age. Meyers added that "in looking back, one is struck by the age's complacency, its self satisfaction with a privileged old order in which the gap between the richest and poorest grew steadily wider". It does not take wild imagination to see the parallels in our time. As the gulf widens between the "haves and have nots" we are sowing the seeds of a future revolution.

Faith does have a positive role. The promise of the Gospel is to offer a new life in Christ replacing self-centeredness in the context of a new community. Recall the two points of biblical law: love God and love neighbor. As to moral authority, look to the Hebrew prophets, e.g. Amos calling out against injustice Look also to Martin Luther who spoke out against religious abuse and today might attack religions of self-esteem. Look also to Martin Luther King, Jr., with whom religion came alive. They all addressed self-interested people indifferent to the needs of the neighbor, especially the underprivileged. Nevertheless, their words came to be recognized as words with moral authority.

---

[4] Karen Bloomquist, "In Today's Context," in *The Promise of Lutheran Ethics,* edited by Karen Bloomquist and John R. Stumme (Fortress Press, 1998), p. 5.

23

Privatization and Globalization

March 28, 2001

Not many years ago the themes of privatization and deregulation were brought into the headlines by Margaret Thatcher and others on the assumption that business could be trusted more than government. Airlines, telephone systems, financial institutions and utilities all changed patterns, supposedly for the benefit of the consumer and, although a great deal of money has changed hands, it has not been always to the benefit of the consumer. Among many of us—whatever we know about economics—these topics can provoke heated discussions. Moreover, it is clear to most of us that short-term efficiencies and corporate profits are not the whole story, as evident in current power shortages. Closely related to these economic issues is the theme of globalization, brought forcefully to our attention with Seattle riots and the University of Oregon's problems with Nike.

Does religion have anything to do with these issues of globalization and economics? The answer is yes, increasingly so. Last month in Davos, Switzerland, a panel of religious leaders faced the World Economic Forum (WEF). It was the first time religious leaders had been invited to an assembly of world leaders in business, science, media and politics. Reporting on the event, Lawrence E. Sullivan, at Harvard Divinity School, wrote that

> Religion has certainly earned a place on this particular stage in recent years. From the Universal Declaration of Human Rights, the dissolution of the Soviet Union...to the Islamic inspirations for radical reform in Iran, Indonesia, and Nigeria, religion has been at the center of modern global affairs. [1]

Sullivan reported that Klaus Schwab, the Swiss business professor who organizes WEF signaled a serious role for religion at the

---

[1] Lawrence E. Sullivan, "Religion on the Global Stage," in *Sightings* (Jonathan Moore, ed), March 7, 2001. Sullivan is director of Harvard Divinity School's Center for the Study of World Religions, which coordinates research on religion and globalization.

conference. Instead of views that religion is "intolerant, irrelevant to economic and political questions, and incapable of understanding global dynamics" participants were made aware of religion's relevance "in stabilizing and legitimizing political and economic systems; in reviving activism in the international system; in mobilizing backlash against globalization's deleterious effects...[and] in providing critical and spiritual reflections from which emerge social, economic, and ecological values". Sullivan wrote that

> Multilateral organizations have never really sought dialogue with religion. The U. N., the World Bank, and the IMF have all avoided dealing directly with religion, but religious institutions dogged the steps of these organizations in Cairo, Beijing, Rio, Kyoto, and Seattle on issues of women, poverty, religious freedom, violence against children, immigration, corruption, refugees, and the environment.

Last year the Lutheran World Federation published a compilation of studies entitled *Justification in the World's Context*, which had been prepared for a previously held consultation seeking new interpretations on the doctrine of justification.[2] Introducing this book, the LWF's General Secretary, Dr. Ishmael Noko, wrote that for Lutherans the theological concept of "justification by grace through faith" is central. But he added an ecumenical note, stating that

> the signing of the Joint Declaration on the Doctrine of Justification...has opened up new interest in the meaning of justification for people today. The Official Common Statement signed by the Lutheran World Federation and the Roman Catholic Church on October 31, 1999 emphasized the need "to interpret the message of justification in language relevant for human beings today, and with reference both to individual and social concerns of our times."

In preparation for the conference at Lutherstadt, Wittenberg, the LWF invited about 50 professors and teachers from Lutheran churches worldwide (30 member churches on six continents) to prepare study papers. With contributions from politics, the sciences, journalism, philosophy and theology, the event was certainly interdisciplinary. A participant from the University of Aarhus (Denmark), Dr. Viggo Mortensen, wrote that

---

[2] Wolfgang Greive (ed.), *Justification in the World's Context*, Documentation No. 45, March 2000, Department for Theology and Studies, Lutheran World Federation (Geneva, Switzerland).

Privatization and Globalization

> The real challenge the church and theology face in the wake of the emergent global culture is the fragmentation of globalized society, and an increasing individualization of religion. Religion is seldom the common voice inviting all, but as a system tends to be diminished and relegated to the margins. In a way, this is strange; from its very origin the church has outstripped modern society in response to globalization because at its basis lies a global vision (cf. Mt 28)... Justification...maintains that we find our identity outside of ourselves.[3]

Although the church does claim a global vision, there was much criticism of globalization, one participant claiming that in current assumptions it has religious overtones and might even be considered a Christian heresy. The question is asked whether economic growth is intrinsically good? How is this affected by the biblical views of stewardship and the integrity of creation? For example, a United Nations' report revealed that the "number of absolute poor has risen to 1.3 billion people–they are chronically undernourished and have no access to clean water. At the same time the 368 billionaires of this world own as much as forty-eight percent of humanity." [4] Along these lines Albérico Baeske, from Brazil, emphasized that "Luther's faith materialized itself in his freedom [which] enables one to become solidary with the oppressed with the necessary celerity and spontaneity."

A startling proposal was suggested by a Canadian that if life in church and society is centered in the theology of the cross and the doctrine of justification, then this "requires not an assimilationist, but a countercultural agenda," that one cannot be comfortable with the god of North American society. [5]

A fitting conclusion is a word from Franklin D. Roosevelt, who in his inaugural address to a dispirited people in 1933 said: "The rulers of the exchange of mankind's goods have failed... They know only the rules of a generation of self-seekers... The measure of the restoration

---

[3] Viggo Mortensen, "Globalization: A Challenge to Theology and the Church," *Justification in the World's Context*, Lutheran World Federation, Documentation No. 45, pp. 48-49.

[4] Wolfgang Kessler, "The effects of the globalized economy on the North and the South," *Justification in the World's Context*, p. 52.

[5] Robert A. Kelly, "Lutheranism as a counterculture? The doctrine of justification and consumer capitalism, " ibid, p. 209.

lies in the extent to which we apply social values more noble than mere monetary profit".

24

The Public Square and the Church

May 18, 2001

Lutheranism claims a tradition of social involvement which can best be understood in its historical perspective. Social concern does not mean simply preaching on morality or social issues nor does it mean that the church becomes a political action platform. It does not mean that the church should build political influence in order to enforce particular views. On the other hand, Lutherans do emphasize a theology of the cross, which in the words of theologian Robert Benne "disallows an optimism that suggests Christians can build the kingdom of God by their energy and will or even that they can discern clearly and confidently what 'God is doing in the world'." Benne contends that

> Lutheran social ethics does not lead in a specific ideological direction, if that is taken to mean a fairly detailed blueprint for public policy. Rather Lutheran ethics provides a framework for doing social ethics or public theology. It elaborates a set of theological assumptions that stipulate how the church and public life ought to be related.[1]

It should be clear that the salvation God offers in Christ is sharply distinguished from any human attempts for a church to build a kingdom or a level of salvation on earth. Benne adds that the church must witness in the public sphere but it is "not primarily a political actor, a social transformer, or an aggressive interest group".

Some religious groups, claiming Scripture as their authority, attempt to build a system of ethics by searching for the passages which will tell one what is right or wrong. Some of the strident voices offering inflexible arguments for particular social issues are not only very selective in skipping and hopping through the Bible looking for proof texts but they use the Bible simply as a book of statutes and then

---

[1] Robert Benne, "Lutheran Ethics: Perennial Themes and Contemporary Challenges," in Karen Bloomquist and John Stumme (eds.), *The Promise of Lutheran Ethics* (Fortress Press, 1998), p. 17. Benne is a professor at Roanoke College, Salem, Virginia.

claim that authority to build their view of God's kingdom. This approach ignores the fact that human beings are a paradox of good and evil and, as Benne noted, are given to "manufacturing idols of the good things they are given". The Bible has a much greater role in the formation of Christian ethics. A professor at the Lutheran School of Theology at Chicago, Reinhold Hütter, has stated that

> Scripture shapes the Christian ethic and becomes its source and norm. First of all, Scripture is the medium in and through which we come to know God, Jesus Christ, the promises of God, and justification. We come to know the interplay of law and gospel, the commandments of God as the way of love in the life of freedom. It's the way in which we get some sense of God's intention *for the world and that toward which we should be striving in our life as disciples*. [2]

In "Models of Ministry," Henry E Horn, a Lutheran pastor and educator, wrote of leadership in the civic space, stating that

> leadership means giving one's skills and energy to those voluntary organizations and ad hoc movements that seek to contribute to the quality of the common life of a city or town. Civic space is here defined as that broad area of community life that lies between our private, individual activities and the larger and formal institutions of our political and economic life... And the end product is not successful church life but a healthy, democratic, improved community life. [3]

Lutherans in America have maintained high regard for the theological heritage in which their concern for the public square is understood within the perspective of the church's mission and the distinctions of law and gospel. The church has been encouraged in this direction by many gifted leaders, such as Franklin Clark Fry, following World War II, who was said to have met with more prime ministers than many national leaders in his insistence that the church must be on the world stage. Another great leader was Frederick H. Knubel, who became a unifying force with the formation of the United Lutheran Church in America in 1918, following the disarray of Lutherans in the previous half-century. Then there was William

---

[2] Reinhard Hütter, "Table Talk," Bloomquist and Stumme (eds.), *Lutheran Ethics*, 161.

[3] Quoted in Frederick K. Wentz, "Birthright Americans: The Shape of the Muhlenberg/Schmucker Tradition," *Seminary Ridge Review*, Summer 1999, p. 13, a publication of the Lutheran Theological Seminary at Gettysburg.

Passavant, who took the lead in establishing institutions of mercy, beginning with a hospital in Pittsburgh in 1849.

These leaders all followed the example of one who is called the patriarch of American Lutheranism, Henry Melchior Muhlenberg, who was intent on planting the church in this frontier soil. Known as the "founder" of organized Lutheranism in the New World, it should be noted that he began his ministry in helping to organize an orphanage. Although Muhlenberg was not actively involved in public life, his three sons present interesting examples of social concern. As described by Frederick K. Wentz,

> All three [of Muhlenberg's sons] began as Lutheran clergy. Peter became a leading general in Washington's army, then entered political life, was vice-president of the Commonwealth of Pennsylvania, member of the first, third, and sixth Congresses, and a United States Senator.
>
> Frederick was a member of the Continental Congress, was twice speaker of the Pennsylvania legislature, was president of the Pennsylvania convention that ratified the federal constitution, was first speaker of the U.S. House of Representatives and again speaker for the third U.S. Congress. Henry, while remaining a pastor in Lancaster, became one of the outstanding botanists of his day... His contributions to the budding nation's first scientific investigations...have been widely recognized by historians. During the early decades of the new United States the three Muhlenbergs were intent on helping to forge a great nation. [4]

Current headlines of news often describe the staunch faith and determination of individuals who commit acts of violence because of an inflexible belief in some ideological position. Frequently such acts are justified by quoting verses from the Bible or biblical interpretations held by various church groups. In contrast Muhlenberg and his sons, as well as other leaders, e.g. Fry, Knubel, and Passavant, did not base their activities on given moral positions, a rigid ideology or a set of commandments. They did not have a Lutheran catalog of do's and don'ts; neither did they use the Bible as a book of regulations. Nevertheless, their faith was clearly reflected in their active social concern.

It would be well to recall an illustration given by Martin Luther in a Christmas sermon in which he said that the Bible was the cradle

---

[4] Frederick K. Wentz, "Birthright Americans," op. cit., p. 17.

which held the Christ child. Unfortunately, some people worship the cradle instead of the Christ within it.

25

Healing in Retribution?

May 29, 2001

The instructions stated that "Prayers may be offered freely by those in the assembly" and a vice surprisingly said, "For Timothy McVeigh". It was the voice of Gail McGrew Eifrig, the editor of *The Cresset*, who described her action a foreword of the journal. Why pray for this man who caused 168 deaths and caused suffering for hundreds of others? Moreover, why pray for one who appears unrepentant and has made no attempt to hide his hatred of government? Eifrig wrote that

> What we hear over and over again as his execution date nears should make us even more sad than these terribly sad deaths and losses. We hear that many people believe that they will find healing in this death. Victims have said that to be healed, they need to know that McVeigh has died. Further, the healing will be more efficacious if they are able to see him die. [1]

We are reminded of passages from Isaiah which we hear on Good Friday and there are attempts to explain the mystery of the atonement but there is no parallel for the Christ as a scapegoat who announced from the cross what was happening. Eifrig quoted Deaconess Louise Williams, who said that "Prayer originates with God and comes from God's incessant desire for relationship with his human children". Requesting a prayer for Timothy McVeigh can be explained as a prayer which rises from God's heart—"the only place where the guilty are still yearned for and desired—and it is given voice within the worshiping community".

In a society which expects its political leaders to be tough on crime, it takes courage to argue against the death penalty. But do we really believe that retributive death will bring healing? I am reminded that in medieval England families would go to a public hanging with

---

[1] Gail McGrew Eifrig, "In Luce Tua," *The Cresset*, May 2001 (Pentecost), pp. 3-4. *The Cresset* is "A review of literature, arts, and public affairs" of Valparaiso University.

a picnic lunch—a family venture. [2] Victims long for healing or closure, to use another popular term, but it will not be found in vengeance or retribution. Healing comes from the victorious Christ and, as Eifrig stated, only making that witness do we locate ourselves at "the place where God's heart for sinners is given voice"—the worshiping community.

Apostolic Succession

Lutherans and Episcopalians (Anglicans) have much in common dating from their distinctive identities, which began in the sixteenth century, but they have always insisted on the broad vision, that they are part of the larger whole, the Church which is one, holy, catholic and apostolic.

In recent decades Lutherans and Episcopalians have taken a number of steps which have brought them closer together, including mutual recognition as churches in which the Gospel is preached and taught (LCA, 1982)! Since 1963 there have been several levels of dialogue both at grass roots and among scholars. An international Anglican-Lutheran dialogue was sponsored by the Lambeth Conference and the Lutheran World Federation (1969-1972). For the Lutheran and Episcopal churches in the United States there was an understanding for the Interim Sharing of the Eucharist. Further steps were intended by which these churches might cooperate in faith and work, although not uniting in administration, proposed in a Concordat of Agreement. This was rejected by the ELCA but later adopted in modified form under the title "Called to Common Mission," which would recognize the authenticity of clergy in both denominations. [3]

A problem for some Lutherans was the insistence that in future ordinations all clergy be brought into the "historic apostolic succession". Although this has been observed in some Lutheran

---

[2] Is there a parallel in the violence of television commercials?

[3] Readings in history are sometimes humorous. In 1986 the Most Rev. Rt. Honorable Robert A. K. Runcie, Archbishop of Canterbury, addressed the convention of the Lutheran Church in America. He noted that relations with the Lutherans were not always amicable: "The English Sovereign rejoices in the August title of Defender of the Faith... This appellation was granted to Henry the VIII by Pope Leo X in 1521 in recognition of the King's defense of the doctrine of the Seven Sacraments over-against what was understood to be Luther's attack. King Henry called Luther a "venomous serpent" and Luther—who rather enjoyed robust controversy—promptly riposted in like serpentine metaphor by calling the King a "deaf adder". (William G. Rusch (ed.), "Address," Dept. for Ecumenical Relations, Lutheran Church in America, 1986.)

churches, in others it has not. Unfortunately, it has become a point of contention. In this context Daniel Malotky, a professor at St. Olaf College, wrote "A Letter to Troubled Lutherans," in which he described a way to overcome the stumbling block by references from St. Paul and Luther. [4] He wrote that Luther did not see any need for insisting on the historic episcopate but that "Luther is not rejecting the episcopate...He is only saying that it is not necessary". Malotky quoted Luther in this context:

> For a Christian as a free man, will say "I will fast, pray, do this and that as men command, not because it is necessary to my righteousness or salvation; but that I may show due respect to the pope, the bishop, the community, a magistrate, or my neighbor, and give them an example. (Luther, "The Freedom of a Christian." Obviously this was written before the break with Rome, but the central point remains the same.) ... Luther advises us to follow the Apostle Paul, who told Christians neither to give human traditions too much weight nor to despise them (Romans 14:13).

Although saved by grace rather than by law, Luther found good reason for Christians to follow the law, as an act of love for the neighbor. Malotky noted that Luther was critical of those who "want to show that they are free men and Christians only be despising and finding fault with ceremonies, traditions, and human laws; as if they were Christians because on stated days they do not fast or eat meat when others fast, or because they do not use the accustomed prayers, and with upturned nose scoff at the precepts of men..." ("The Freedom of the Christian").

Those who oppose "Called to Common Mission" have had much to say about the 16th century Lutheran confessions, the historical documents of Lutheranism. But it should be remembered that the Augsburg Confession, a principal document, was written in the hope of reconciliation, not a basis for independence. Lutherans desiring theological rectitude and Episcopalians observing tradition have much to learn from each other as well as a practical need for a shared ministry in various parts of the country.

---

[4] Daniel Malotky, "A Letter to Troubled Lutherans," *The Cresset,* May 2001 (Pentecost), pp. 10-11.

26

A Focus on Pain and Reaction

September 15, 2001

Television, radio and newspapers have been remarkably effective in reporting, probing and analyzing the terrorist attacks which have shaken the nation this past week. There was intense coverage of the what, where, when and who but very little focus on the why. Turning away from the repeated images of dramatic effect, I longed for print forms of "in depth" comments on the "why" but these have been scarce.

One letter to the editor asked poignantly "why some people would hate us so much". As though in answer columnist Thomas Friedman wrote in the next page that this assault is not from another superpower but from angry men and women, many of whom "hail from failing states in the Muslim and Third World" where they

> resent America's influence over their lives, politics and children, not to mention our support for Israel...And think of what they hit: the World Trade Center—the beacon of American led capitalism that both tempts and repels them, and the Pentagon, the embodiment of American military superiority. [1]

The columnist added that a serious and respectful dialogue with the Muslim world is needed. Moreover, writing from Jerusalem, he said the United States should not ignore Palestinian concerns and in spite of their grievances America is their best ray of hope. Friedman noted that the U.S. plan presented at Camp David "may not be sufficient for Palestinians". From Cairo, Egypt, for the Associated Press Donna Bryson reported on other attitudes toward the United States:

> Some said they rejoiced that the United States was learning a lesson in suffering. Others condemned the celebrations in refugee camps. She quoted Gamal Nkrumah, a Cairo writer [who said] "A lot of people feel that the U.S. couldn't care less about the suffering of three

---
[1] Thomas Friedman, "Fighting a super-empowered angry horde" (*New York Times*), *The Oregonian*, Sep. 14, 2001.

Healing in Retribution? 81

quarters of mankind". Few Americans would recognize the portrait of their country in places such as En-el-Hilweh, a Palestinian refugee camp gripped by poverty... [Its] 70,000 residents blame America's military and diplomatic support for Israel for preventing them from returning to homes they or their parents fled when the Jewish state was founded in 1948. [2]

Referring to the Israeli-Palestinian focus, there were two items in The Oregonian which had reference to Lutherans in that area, a recognition, incidentally, that a significant minority of the Palestinians is Christian. One item is a quotation from Mitri Raheb, pastor of Christmas Evangelical Lutheran Church in Bethlehem, West Bank:

> As Palestinians, we can very well understand the pain of our American friends. We know what it means when political leaders are targeted and are not safe in their own offices. We understand what it means when planes attack security headquarters. We know how it feels when the backbone of the economy is assaulted. [3]

The second item was a color picture on the front page of the Lutheran Church in Beit Jalla, West Bank, with Israeli tanks rolling by in front. The article stated that "Israeli troops seized part of a predominantly Christian Palestinian town despite international criticism".

American reaction to the terrorist attacks have been variously described with such words as horror, disgust, anger, sadness. Because these reactions are understandable the words of Portland's Rabbi Emanuel Rose should be taken to heart:

> In times of tragedy anger is normal, and it is common to seek short-term solace in a mood of retaliation. We do hope that our government will move wisely, but with absolute determination to eliminate global terrorism. [4]

---

[2] Donna Bryson, "Arab world views attacks," Associated Press, *The Oregonian,* Sep. 12, 2001.

[3] Mitri Raheb quoted in "Voices," *The Oregonian,* Sep. 13, 2001. Sudarsan Raghaven, "Israeli forces seize part of town in West Bank," Knight Ridder News, *The Oregonian,* Aug. 29, 2001.

[4] Rabbi Emanuel Rose, "Scars fade, hearts heal, and our nation will rebound proudly," *Portland Tribune,* Sep. 14, 2001

To accomplish Rabbi Rose's goal requires the recognition that, although a superpower, the United States is nevertheless a part of the world community and our concern must necessarily be for the well being of all humanity. It demands perspective but are we Americans able to look dispassionately at ourselves? A friend at St. James told of a phone call from neighbors who had been unable to return home because of the grounding of airliners. Stranded in Dresden, Germany, they mentioned the deeply felt sympathy and empathy expressed by their German friends. I could not help think that the people of Dresden would have every right to anger toward Americans because of the firebombing of Dresden during World War II. It was highly controversial at the time because there was no military significance to that beautiful and historically rich city. If everyone in Hitler's Germany was culpable, what about office workers in the World Trade Buildings? Nevertheless, the horror remains in our hearts.

It is difficult and uncomfortable to be personally self-critical. Moreover, one has to be determined to rise above horror and anger while continuing to wave our flag and yet to ask again why there are so many people in the world who hate us? Undoubtedly there are some who are simply envious of the rich and the powerful. On the other hand, has there not been an insensitivity toward others? Many examples come to mind. The United States is the greatest culprit in global warming but we refused to sign or discuss the Kyoto accord. Similarly we have gone our own way regarding land mines and germ warfare. In the United Nations even our allies go against us and the United States and Israel have had the distinction of casting the only negative votes, with the result that we withhold our dues. As to terrorism, recall our support of the Contras in Central America. In economic matters, repeatedly we have been told that America (and Europe) lives richly off the resources of the third world countries.

It has been said that after Tuesday the world is vastly different. We need to recognize that we are part of a world community and that the profit motif must be tempered with calm consideration of social pressures. Security is necessary but we must be determined to remain a free and open society. Words of Kathleen Dean Moore, a professor of philosophy at Oregon State University, wrote about her concern:

> And you know what I'm most afraid of? I'm afraid Americans will not be able to bear the silence. I'm terrified that we will rush to fill

the breathless pause with action and noise—with whistling bombs and angry politicians, with the clatter of dollars poured into defense, gunning engines, oil wells furiously pounding, the noise of an angry nation on the march to war against the vague illusive world. [5]

As a nation, we are not dismayed. Clearly evident is our inner strength and the resolve to overcome the pain of these tragic actions. Thus we can proudly wave our flags, not in blind anger, but with calm determination to follow high ideals.

---

[5] Kathleen Dean Moore, "An ode to evil," *The Oregonian,* Sep. 12, 2001.

27

Government No Longer the Enemy

September 18, 2001

Dag Hammarskjold
 The terrorist assaults of September 11 have not only had worldwide repercussions but they have forcefully demonstrated the necessity of global thinking. Thus it is appropriate to recognize the day of commemoration for Dag Hammarskjold, this eighteenth of September. Highly regarded for his work with the United Nations, it is clear that he wrestled with the "reality of the Christian revelation and its implications for his life". According to one description, he "combined secular work, primarily diplomatic service, with a deep desire for personal spirituality...[as expressed in his Markings:] 'In our era, the road to holiness necessarily passes through the world of action'." [1]

Government is no longer the enemy
 Ronald Reagan's famous statement that "government is the enemy" is no longer in vogue. In the horrors of a Tuesday morning America looked immediately to government for leadership, for stabilizing strength and for an expression of positive hope. For decades it has been popular for political figures to run against government, against Washington. Obviously, the whole nation has suddenly recognized our national strength in government during this past week.
 President Bush himself is a case in point. Americans are now looking to him for leadership and it is apparent that he and his administration are making every effort to fill that role. Commentator John Balzar wrote about great ironies:

> We elected a president on the narrowest of grounds. Tax rates, drug prices, school exams. We voted for someone to manage government. We received an ideologue on a mission to cut it. Now he must command it. Great events create great ironies. Ours is this: Bush was the man of the moment for those whose faith in government had

---
[1] Philip Pfatteicher, *Festivals and Commemorations,* Augsburg, 1980, pp. 359-360.

ebbed. He stood apart from Washington. The moment changed. All eyes turn to Washington where the federal government is central to our shaken lives. We no longer want a president apart, but on top. Now we rally around this president or around our hopes for him. Unseasoned in diplomacy. Uninspiring as an orator. Unimposing to the camera. An un-president for millions of Americans. Destiny handed him the summons... We wait to learn what he is made of. [2]

The president's popularity has risen and it has been said that he has grown during this week of tragedy. Apart from partisan loyalties, there are many who want him to be an effective leader for the good of the nation. But there is a risk in that it might be tempting for him to act on widespread anger. This was evident in some excerpts The Oregonian printed from the British press, such as a blunt quote from the Guardian: "The American people need a statesman, but they want a cowboy". The New York Times sounded a cautionary note in stating that "Bellicose rhetoric from George W. Bush did nothing to calm the market's jitters" and "cowboy-style rhetoric like his 'wanted dead or alive' remark does not add to the war against terrorism". [3]

It is to President Bush's credit that he spoke against Jerry Falwell and Pat Robertson's recent comments that God had allowed the terrorists to succeed because the United States had become a "nation of abortion, homosexuality, secular schools and courts, and the American Civil Liberties Union". [4] Robertson had invited Falwell to his television program and said in response: "I totally concur". Bush's rejection of that comment is significant because he (and the GOP) has received much support from the religious right wing and Falwell, as at the National Cathedral's memorial service at the president's invitation.

Another point of irony in the new respect for government is that the airlines are seeking a "government bailout of between $10 billion and $20 billion [and at] the same time, carriers and industry experts say the burden of providing security for the industry should be shifted to a federal agency," a plan which Delta executive Leo F.

---

[2] John Balzar, "From a foxhole, Americans watch to see where Bush leads," (Los Angeles Times), *The Oregonian*, Sept. 16, 2001.

[3] Editorial, *New York Times*, Sept. 18, 2001.

[4] Laurie Goodstein, "Falwell's Finger-Pointing Inappropriate, Bush says," *New York Times*, Sept. 15, 2001.

Mullin said he and his colleagues favored. [5] How strange this sounds against the familiar themes of the last decades, that private enterprise is more effective and less expensive than government. The old themes of privatization and deregulation have to overcome the evidence of airline operations and their recent record of power and energy crises. As to the bailout, the airlines are clearly part of our transportation network, although an old refrain comes to mind: "Let the market place handle it". [6]

The president's emphasis on a war footing brings to mind a warning by columnist Anthony Lewis, who wrote that we re fighting an elusive enemy and there is danger that "military action would trigger the Law of Unintended Consequences... Afghanistan is a prime example. When the Soviet Union invaded there in 1979, the United States armed Islamic forces to resist. The country ended up in the hands of anti-Western extremists". [7] Might our own weapons be used against us? Unintended consequences have also been noted in the president's use of the word "crusade," which elicited Steve Duin's recent visit with history: "We will rid the world of evil-doers:

> So said the president Sunday. So goes the crusade.
> As it's been several centuries since the good guys embarked on a holy war, I'm not sure which number we're on. If you've lost count, the First Crusade to free us from the yoke of Islamic fundamentalism was launched in 1096 and eventually led to the conquest of Jerusalem. The Second Crusade went nowhere. The Third Crusade, with an 1189 kickoff, was the one Richard the Lionhearted funded with the "Saladin tithe," a 25% tax on all the Jews in England. The Fourth Crusade was redirected by Doge Enrico Dandolo of Venice into the muderous sack of Constantinople, the Eastern capital of Christianity.
> And let's not forget the Albigensian Crusade... When the various mercenaries who "took the Cross" complained to Count Simon of Monfort that they were having a tough time weeding out the heretics from the ordinary Frenchmen, Simon replied, "Kill them all. God

---

[5] Jim Krane, "Airlines seek help staying aloft," Associated Press, *The Oregonian,* Sep. 17, 2001. As to bailouts by the government, recall the savings and loan industry and federal money backing Chrysler's recover. Government has not always been an "enemy".

[6] Why not build up the neglected railroad system for the short and medium runs, letting the airlines handle long distance? Railroads should be major people movers because they are convenient, less expensive and less damaging ecologically than air travel and freeways.

[7] Anthony Lewis, "U.S. must plot a mighty, but measured response," *The Oregonian,* Sept. 16, 2001.

will know his own". The devout crusaders complied, slaughtering 26,000 people, barely a handful of the 1 million who died during that crusade.

Small wonder Steven Runciman described the tragic destructiveness of the Crusades with the epitaph: "There was so much courage and so little honour, so much devotion and so little understanding". [8]

---

[8] Steve Duin, "We will rid the world of evil-doers," *The Oregonian*, Sep. 18, 2001.

28

Views from New Zealand

November 22, 2001

Preparations were made long in advance. Sandra and I were to leave for New Zealand on September 13. However, events in New York on September 11 changed our plans. Just two hours before we intended to walk to the Square to ride Max to the airport we were told that the trip would be postponed. A couple weeks later we did, in fact, make the trip, enjoying it thoroughly. [1]

Throughout the trip I picked up all the newspapers I could find and in my customary manner clipped items of interest. The terrorist attacks on New York were in every paper and they had extensive coverage during the length of our stay. Of great interest to me were the editorials and the columns on the opinion pages and I was eager for perspectives from outside the U.S. All of the newspapers were full of articles on terrorism and public support was clearly for aid to the U.S. but the papers decried America's unilateralism. For example, the U.S. rejection of the Kyoto accord on global warming was still in the news. Now, a couple months later, selected clippings from those New Zealand papers are spread out in front of me and the key word "perspective" comes to mind. The quotations below serve as illustrations.

Particularly appealing to me were the poignant remarks of an American expatriate, Dr. William Shepard, a professor in Religious Studies at the University of Canterbury, whose remarks at a panel on the U.S. crisis were printed in Christchurch's newspaper.

> I am an American, a loyal American, and I believe in America, but of course, I make some distinctions. The America I believe in and am loyal to is not the America that built itself on the twin pillars of the slavery of blacks and the genocide of natives, but the America that was conceived in liberty and dedicated to the proposition that all people are created equal.

---
[1] We had an extensive tour of both the North and South Islands in the company of people mostly from Britain and Australia. Our impressions are simply stated: if we had to choose another place to live, New Zealand would be at the top of the list.

The America I believe in and am loyal to is not the America of know-nothings and rednecks but the America that has created... an increasingly pluralist society...
It is not the America of McCarthyite frenzy, although it is the America that fought and defeated Nazism and communism. It is not the America of the military-industrial complex and the arrogance of power that destroyed Vietnamese villages in order to save them, that connived at dictatorships and destabilised popular regimes in Latin America... It is the America which has protested and demonstrated against all this, not always without effect.

My loyalty goes to the President when he says in the present situation: "No-one should be singled out for unfair treatment, or unkind words, because of their ethnic background or religious faith," particularly when he says this...from inside a mosque. But I am much less loyal when he simplistically tells all other nations "Either you are with us, or you are with the terrorists".

Americans ask: "Why do they hate us?" Traveling in the Third World I have often wondered why they do not hate us more—why, in fact, they seem to love us at least as much as they hate us. I believe they love us for those aspects of America to which I can give my loyalty. [2]

For another perspective, Robert Harris, a writer from London contrasted the leadership of Tony Blair and George W. Bush, noting a reversal of roles.

I have always found something inherently alarming about states run by Presidents. I'm fundamentally uneasy about all the psychodrama that seems to go with the presidential system: the "lonely leader" guff, the motorcades, the personal physician, the unelected chiefs of staff... The events of September 11 at first reinforced this prejudice... That such a slight man should be occupying such an immense office at such a perilous time seemed to be the stuff of nightmares, making one more thankful than ever to live in a parliamentary democracy here in Britain, in which no single individual's finger rested on the trigger and in which power was diffused across the executive.

But something very strange has happened over the past three weeks. Gradually it has become apparent that America is the country run by a cabinet of powerful equals, in which the leader is essentially

---

[2] William Shepard, "America's chance to be good and great," *The Press* (Christchurch), Oct. 12, 2001. Shepard's reference to the "genocide of natives" reminds me that the two AnglicanAnglican church services I attended incorporated some Maori language in the common liturgy. At Auckland the congregation sang the Lord's Prayer in Maori.

> primus inter pares... It is Britain that looks like the presidential state... To most people's surprise, Prime Minister Bush has emerged... One gets the impression of something like genuine cabinet government. President Blair has also emerged well from the emergency. But unlike Prime Minister Bush, he has done it by dispensing with his cabinet colleagues [who have] met only once since the crisis started. [3]

Although Harris was uneasy about Blair's role, another writer, David Aaronovitch, wrote that "Tony Blair picks up where Churchill left off". Referring to one of Blair's speeches, Aaronovich said that for him "this was the most exhilarating and internationalist address by a British political leader since Winston Churchill roamed the post war scene". For example, the reporter stated,

> The key phrase was this: "Out of the shadow of this evil should emerge lasting good." Because, as Blair implied, we cannot go on living like this. [Also,] this fragility makes internationalism sensible. Or, in his words, "self interest and mutual interest are inextricably woven together" in an interdependent world... Can you imagine Margaret Thatcher saying that, if the Rwandan massacres were to happen again, we would have a moral duty to act there also? [4]

Yet another writer, Chris Trotter, wrote appreciatively of Blair, noting that he was not simply showing solidarity with the Americans but was broadening the view, "reaching out to "the starving, the wretched, the dispossessed, the ignorant, those living in want and squalor from the deserts of northern Africa to the slums of Gaza, to the mountain ranges of Afghanistan: they too are our cause". Trotter's compelling point: "Until I hear more compassionate and persuasive words, I am—and will remain—under Tony Blair's spell". [5]

Although overwhelming support to aid the United States was apparent, there was nevertheless some criticism, such as a column from a Dunedin student, who wrote to President Bush:

---

[3] Robert Harris, "President Blair, Prime Minister Bush," Telegraph Group Ltd, *New Zealand Herald*, Oct. 4, 2001.

[4] David Aaronovitch, "'War leader' imposes his moral authority on all," *New Zealand Herald*, Oct. 4, 2001.

[5] Chris Trotter, "Falling under Tony Blair's spell," *The Dominion*, Oct. 5, 2001.

Views from New Zealand

Dear George: There are no overnight solutions to terrorism. But there are things you could do. How about joining the International Criminal Court? Supporting distribution of food? ... And most of all, how about a real in-depth analysis of American foreign policy in the 20th century. Perhaps you could work out a new approach for the 21st century—e.g. stop going into countries and screwing them over.[6]

Looking ahead with a positive outlook, the following quotation from Dr. Shepard is certainly appropriate:

> I believe that the United States is the greatest nation today... Greatness is not goodness, of course, and I cannot agree with the claim of former President Eisenhower when he said: "America is great because she is good". I believe that America has done as well as any at mixing goodness with power, but I want to see her do better. With the terrible events of September 11, we face a new challenge to our leadership role.

---

[6] Melanie Bunce, "Dear George—don't get even, get thinking," *Otago Daily Times*, Oct. 12, 2001.

29

Authoritarianism and the War on Terror

November 25, 2001

The September 11 attack was a wake-up call, the sudden recognition that the peace and normalcy Americans had taken for granted were not, in fact, secure. The conservative unilateralists in this Bush administration who had been disengaged from the world were suddenly faced with a multilateral challenge. Americans in their complacency had chosen not to see the globalized turmoil in the growing divisions between the rich and poor nations. As one writer noted, the "Americanized global system...generated a great mass of discontents". [1]

Referring to that day of terror, Dr. Timothy Lull, president of Pacific Lutheran Theological Seminary, spoke of a new opportunity: "I am proud of the churches and the role they played in bringing people together for comfort and hope in a time of great national sadness. It seemed a real moment of spiritual opportunity." [2] Asking how we can "sustain the good that was done," he suggested that our greatest need is to understand the faiths of our non-Christian neighbors.

Christianity, Judaism and Islam, three monotheistic religions have all been involved in warfare and it would be wrong to stereotype any of them. The current struggle has been called a war against terrorism but columnist Thomas Friedman has written that

> Terrorism is just a tool. We're fighting to defeat an ideology: religious totalitarianism. World War II and the cold war were fought to defeat secular totalitarianism—Nazism and Communism—and World War III is a battle against religious totalitarianism, a view of the world

---

[1] Michael Hirsh in a book review of David Halberstam, *War in a Time of Peace* (Scribner's), *Foreign Affairs*, November/December 2001, p. 161.

[2] Timothy F. Lull, *Span* (a publication of Pacific Lutheran Theological Seminary), Autumn, 2001.

that my faith must reign supreme... It has to be fought in schools, mosques, churches and synagogues. [3]

News accounts have reported the fanaticism of some of the foreign soldiers fighting for the Taliban, noting that many have been trained in fundamentalist schools, although they remain illiterate. Such schools have not featured the A B C's but have implanted an ideology. Christians and Jews have also made use of fundamentalist schools, teaching a vision of an exclusive religion. Friedman added that the opposite of religious totalitarianism is an ideology of pluralism, "an ideology that embraces religious diversity...without claiming exclusive truth".

Under fundamentalism, which can be political as well as religious, all aspects of life are subject to a single view. There is an arrogance in the claim that the "totality" of history and the intentions of God are wrapped up in one view applicable in the present moment and that the true believer possesses that view. Were faith and scripture irrelevant for generations past? Christian and Jewish fundamentalists continue to this day the debate on recognition of alternative faiths. When fundamentalists argue for prayer in the schools, are they thinking of a Mormon prayer in Utah or a Buddhist prayer in San Francisco? Fundamentalist Jews in Israel have a record opposing secular trends. Friedman claimed that although Christianity and Judaism have struggled with this issue for centuries, Islam has not developed a view which "allows equal recognition of alternative faith communities". Another writer describes the issue:

> Worldwide, Muslims are engaged in an enduring struggle to maintain a religious identity and culture while confronting the economic, social and political forces of Westernization. This is true both in places left behind, like Afghanistan, and in more industrialized Asian nations like Indonesia and Malaysia. [4]

Yet there have been times in which Muslim societies were advanced. For example, in the dark ages when Christians were burning the writings of Greek philosophers, Muslims retained that heritage. And medical students, hampered by Christian restrictions, would sometimes go to Muslim cities for their studies. Now that worldwide

---

[3] Thomas L. Friedman, "The Real War," *New York Times*, November 27, 2001.

[4] Eric Talmadge, "West wrong to stereotype Muslims," *Otago Daily Times*, October 8, 2001, once again quoting from a New Zealand paper.

attention is focused on Islam, one can hope that there will be such interpretations of the Islamic heritage as to see their future in a globalized world.

The problem of a narrow authoritarian and exclusivist order is evident in the excess of the Taliban, which is said to have started with actions of good will by students of religion. But it grew to be a monster of oppression. Such monsters have developed also in other areas—with Hitler on the right and Stalin on the left, their methods identical. Shortly after World War II, Hannah Arendt wrote a study of totalitarianism in which she referred to their popular support:

> Nothing is more characteristic of the totalitarian movement in general...than the startling swiftness with which they are forgotten and the startling ease with which they can be replaced... It would be a still more serious mistake to forget, because of this impermanence, that the totalitarian regimes, so long as they are in power, and the totalitarian leaders, so long as they re alive, "command and rest upon mass support" up to the end. Hitler's rise to power was legal in terms of majority rule and neither he nor Stalin could have maintained the leadership of large populations...if they had not had the confidence of the masses. [5]

The current progress of the "war against terrorism" has the support of the nation but there is danger in eroding basic rights with anti-terrorist legislation. Extraordinary powers need effective oversight. Some of us recall the days when J. Edgar Hoover was a hero and now we recognize that no president was secure enough to replace him. The abuses of the McCarthy years brought ruin to thousands of Americans. Currently, how many people are now held in detention with no charges filed and no access to legal help? Are we to speed up "justice" with military-style courts? Vice-president Cheney is quoted as saying, "Don't worry. It's not for U.S. citizens".

A better understanding of our neighbors is needed and locally the current lecture series at St. James is attracting deserved attention. Moreover, we should recognize the extent that our lives affect other people around the globe. Made aware again of the poor and needy in the world, Dr. Lull reminds us that we have strong resources in our church through the Lutheran World Federation, which is able "to do good credibly and efficiently even at a great distance".

---

[5] Hannah Arendt, *Totalitarianism*, (Harcourt, Brace & World), pp. 3-4. Note the objections—on the basis of patriotism—of Portland's rank and file police to the caution of city leaders regarding sweeping interrogations of people from the Middle East.

30

Bonhoeffer's Warning of Fascism

December 6, 2001

As we find ourselves engaged in an unofficial war, the story of Dietrich Bonhoeffer has particular bearing. A Lutheran pastor in Germany who had gained widespread recognition as a theologian, Bonhoeffer was conspicuous in his opposition to the power assumed by Hitler. He recognized a church-state conflict at the time of the installation of Adolf Hitler as chancellor on January 30, 1933. Just two days later Bonhoeffer gave a radio address in which he warned that the leadership principles (Führer-Prinzip) would lead to idolatry. The extent of Hitler's power at that early date was evident in that Bonhoeffer was cut off the air in the middle of his address.

Generally known that Hitler's steps to power were legal, it should be noted that he was widely popular. He was leading Germany out of its humiliation and the devastating effects of the years after the First World War. Leadership and power were clearly his. But a succession of events in 1933 drew attention to the state-church struggle. Two months after Hitler became chancellor Jews were dismissed from public offices. In July there were church elections which placed more than 70% of the Deutsche Christen under the notorious Reichsbischoff L. Müeller. Whole companies of storm troops were led into church services, both to please and frighten the churches.

Bonhoeffer's story continued. While teaching in Union Seminary, New York, against the advice of his friends, he decided to return to Germany. Lutherans there were struggling with their sense of patriotism and their religious faith until there was a split and an underground church was formed. Bonhoeffer formed a clandestine seminary. The story of his active opposition to Hitler is well known and Bonhoeffer was hanged a day before U.S. troops captured the prison. He died a martyr but his influence continues, as in the "cost of discipleship," in which he made a distinction between "cheap" and costly grace. Cheap grace, he wrote, was communion without confession or forgiveness without repentance. In true grace there would be the resultant of suffering, discipline and obedience. But for the purpose of this paper, Bonhoeffer's resistance to the idolatry of authoritarian figures should be noted.

The surge of patriotism following the attacks of September 11 reveals overwhelming support for our government in the war against terrorism. Moreover, the progress of the military campaign to date has been so successful that there has been a flush of enthusiasm to expand the war to other countries, although it should be clear that the post-military phase of the war may be much more difficult. [1] It has been said that winning a war does not mean winning the peace, which is won only only through hearts and minds.

The patriotic wave has lowered the voices of those who considered government an enemy but unfortunately there is a danger of losing balance. *The New York Times* printed a lengthy editorial on "War and the Constitution," noting that the country "wants very much to be supportive of the war on terrorism and is finding it hard to summon up much outrage" over the extraordinary powers the Bush administration is assuming but added a caution: "The extreme nature of these new measures and the arbitrary way in which they were adopted are stirring a growing uneasiness among both Republicans and Democrats in Congress, as well as America's overseas allies." [2] News reports have highlighted the balance-of-powers struggle between Senator Patrick Leahy, chairman of the Senate Judiciary Committee and Attorney General John Ashcroft, in which Leahy has stated that as an American and a Vermonter he wants to see us protected from terrorism but he wants it done in a way that does "not diminish the basic protections of the Constitution".

Regarding the extraordinary powers, the *Times'* editorial stated that the "administration has awarded itself some of these powers, which go well beyond those just granted in the anti-terrorism legislation Congress approved". Included is the intention to allow the FBI to spy on domestic religious and political groups without probable cause, which brings to mind numerous abuses in the 1960s and 1970s. Also in the *Times'* editorial:

---

[1] "While those in the Bush administration spoiling for a regional war have not prevailed, the situation is congenial to lunatic ideas. *The Wall Street Journal* recently featured the conservative historian Paul Johnson calling explicitly for colonizing the entire region. Leaving aside the arrogance of the idea, does any sane person think that...millions of Arabs or Muslims would sit still for nineteenth-century occupation?"—Robert Kuttner, "No Ordinary Time," *The American Prospect*, Nov. 5, 2001.

[2] Editorial, *The New York Times*, Dec. 2, 2001. Following quotations are from this source.

One of the most troubling moves by the administration has been the secret and in some cases prolonged detention of suspects... The American system does not hold with the idea of incarcerating a large group of people who it seems to have no credible reason to believe are dangerous.

Another dangerous step is the president's decision to authorize military tribunals. Arguments have been raised that this move lacks Congressional authorization, that they "trespass on the separation of powers," that they can be held in secret, and that they are not limited to prisoners overseas.

> The order's breadth is astonishing, allowing for the indefinite incarceration and trial of any non-citizen the president deems...to be involved in international terrorism of any type or to be harboring terrorists. After Sept. 11, Americans were introduced to any number of homeowners who sheltered the men who were about to become hijackers, with no realization they were anything but students. The scope of these powers should make the potential for abuse clear.

Another danger is that non-citizens are being deprived of civil liberties, thus creating a parallel system of law. The right to a fair trial, to consult with a lawyer (without government wiretaps), and protection against lengthy and secret detention should not be for American citizens only. One class of people should not be considered unworthy of basic human rights. The conservative writer William Safire leaves no doubt on these issues:

> Misadvised by a frustrated and panic-stricken Attorney General, a president of the United States has just assumed what amounts to dictatorial power to jail or execute aliens. In his infamous emergency order, Bush admits to dismissing "the principles of law and the rules of evidence" that undergird America's system of justice. He seizes the power to circumvent the courts and set up his own drumhead tribunals... Bush now strips the alien accused of even the limited rights afforded by a court martial. His kangaroo court can conceal evidence by citing national security... [3]

The message of Dietrich Bonhoeffer is clear.

---

[3] William Safire, "Our fears shouldn't trump the Constitution" (*New York Times*), *The Oregonian*, Nov. 16, 2001.

31

"Between Vision and Reality"

December 8, 2001

Back in November, 1998, Pastor Smith invited me to write an occasional page for St. James' newsletter. For some years previous I had been writing my little pages of comments on political, social or churchly matters, perhaps as a means of venting steam, and mailing them to family and friends. Pastor Smith had been receiving these commentaries and suggested that a continuation of such themes, would be appropriate in the parish newsletter. He suggested that they might appear once a month, to which I agreed, subject to the Muse's inspiration or retirement's heavy demands.

To my surprise this is the 31st issue of "Musings" and to my greater surprise there has been no serious negative criticism. Because I cannot imagine that everyone is in agreement with what I write, it probably means that the members of St. James are exceedingly gentle and polite or—more likely—this page is not read. I have made no attempt for balance in themes and there is no index for these papers. These writings are simply the observations of a churchman who is much concerned about the world in which we live—thus the subjects are necessarily social and political.

In the early years of my ministry I had very little interest in these matters, thinking simplistically that society would improve when individual attitudes improved, not recognizing then that we are necessarily related to families, congregations, and communities. My first parish was in St. Thomas, Virgin Islands, and my concern, as a very young pastor, was not to be overwhelmed by the responsibility of suddenly caring for a congregation with rich traditions, reaching back to 1666. Next I found myself in Las Vegas, Nevada, engaged in organizing a new congregation. It was several years later, during the construction of the church building, that I became increasingly conscious of the concerns of a community of faith. [1] Sunday morning

---

[1] Influential for me was a little book by Edward Trail Horn, *Altar and Pew* (United Lutheran Church in America).

worship is not a number of individuals engaged in individual devotions but individuals with personal faith who are working together for purpose—in a sense, teamwork—all coming to a focus in liturgical action. It was of great importance therefore to understand and learn how to use the instruments of liturgy, which had been meaningful to people of faith over the centuries. Clearly, an entertainment-style of worship would appear hollow and superficial, especially so in Las Vegas. The liturgy, on the other hand, has effectively served people of many cultures and ethnic backgrounds for countless generations.

Words of the Creed took on new meanings, such as the four marks of the church: "We believe in one holy catholic and apostolic church". Moreover, a critical part of our heritage is the evangelical center, the good news (gospel) of Jesus Christ. Back when our Evangelical Lutheran Church in America was being formed there was discussion regarding the name. Some of us who were not in the center of action thought that a good name might be "Evangelical Catholic". Of course, "it would never fly," but consider the theoretical understanding of the words—its heart in the gospel (evangel) with a catholic (universal) breadth and purpose.

A recent publication of the Lutheran World Federation has the title *Between Vision and Reality: Lutheran Churches in Transition*.[2] This 500 page volume is a collection of essays and findings, the result of a three-year study program to determine how the church understands itself in our changing times. In other words, what is our identity? Where are we going? The book contains essays and findings from consultations held over three years on five continents, meeting in Chemnai, India; Moshi, Tanzania; São Leopoldo, Brazil; Chicago, USA; and Lund, Sweden. In a descriptive summary, the committee made this statement:

> The church's struggle for identity is faced with several major tensions that are intertwined and interrelated: inclusiveness versus tribal, racial, and ethnic exclusiveness; unity of faith in Christ versus ecclesial and cultural plurality, openness to the world versus a mentality of self-sufficiency; the basic belief of being saved by grace alone versus church efforts at self-justification by efficiency, growth, and prosperity. In sum, the Lutheran church is caught in and struggling

---

[2] Wofgang Greive (ed.) *Between Vision and Reality: Lutheran Churches in Transition*, Lutheran World Federation, Documentation 2001/47, Geneva, Switzerland.

with, many new forms of the perennial tension between its confession and its contextuality. ³

Recognizing that on all continents there has been a loss of traditional community, societies are forced to deal with basic questions of orientation. Therefore, at the consultations theological discussion could not ignore the social sciences. Historical examples were mentioned in that Martin Luther and Johannes Bugenhagen prepared new church orders and structures of community life, "there being no inherent conflict between justification and justice, spiritual and social community, service in the church and service in the world". ⁴

It was also clear that within Lutheranism there is "a renewed awareness of the centrality of worship in the Christian faith... rediscovering the relevance of signs, symbols, and rites." An affirmation regarding the Gospel and the Church stated:

> The witness of this church in society flows from its identity as a community that lives from and for the gospel. Faith is active in love; love calls for justice in the relationships and structures of society. It is in grateful response to God's grace in Jesus Christ that this church carries out its responsibility for the well-being of society and the environment.
>
> Word and Sacrament are the originating center for this church's mission in the world. [Moreover,] as a reconciling and healing presence, this church is called to minister to human need with compassion and imagination... As a prophetic presence, this church has the obligation to name and denounce the idols before which people bow, to identify the power of sin present in social structures, and to advocate in hope with poor and powerless people. ⁵

Among current changes in our world, it was noted that there is a new turning to religion, a new interest in the power of the spirit which influences a group or an individual, a new interest in the healing power of religion. The solid affirmation of these studies by the Lutheran World Federation is that Lutheranism is part of the "one holy catholic and apostolic" Church.

---

¹¹ *Between Vision and Reality*, p. 24.

¹² *Between Vision and Reality,* p. 18.

¹³ *Between Vision and Reality*, p. 213-215.

An International Church

June 27, 2002

This summer the Sunday School at St. James is taking a world tour by way of pictures and descriptions of the church in other lands. Next to the Roman Catholic Church, the Lutheran Church is perhaps the most international of churches. Because I had once visited Lutheran churches in Poland, I was invited to show some of the pictures to the Sunday School class.

The Oregon Synod of the ELCA is linked as a companion church with the Lutheran Church in Poland, which is known as the Church of the Augsburg Confession. In the fall of 1995 Oregon Synod's Bishop Paul Swanson led a delegation to visit the companion church in Poland. Privileged to be included in this delegation, the visit strengthened my belief that a Christian must be increasingly aware of a global context, and furthermore, that the church, reaching across national lines is a marvelous instrument for expressing discipleship.

In Warsaw the delegation met with Polish Lutheran Bishop Jan Szarek, who described the church he served. He said that Lutherans in Poland once numbered over two million persons but now counted about 100,000 for various reasons, such as changing national boundaries and the movement, forced or voluntary, of large portions of the population. With this background and recognizing that Lutherans are a minority (although the largest minority) next to Roman Catholics in Poland, one might expect to see a demoralized church with a defeatist attitude. This, however, was certainly not the case. In a tight schedule our delegation visited thirty some parishes and various institutions of the Church of the Augsburg Confession. Pastors and lay people throughout the visit reflected a bold confidence, which looked not to the past but to the future.

This forward-looking attitude was reflected in conversations during a visit to one of the church's care centers. One could imagine the numerous heart-rending stories which might be told by the residents regarding the last half-century. This was a time marked by invading armies first from the west and then from the east, vast destruction (80% of Warsaw destroyed) and the dislocation and separation of many families through population movements. Imagine the countless instances of hunger and pain. There was also the strain of living under different forms of government, from brief independence to right-wing fascism to left-wing communism and once again to open elections. In all of our visits there was no hint of the "poor little us" syndrome.

An example of the international context of the church was forcefully evident to us at Sunday's worship in Warsaw's Lutheran Church of the Holy Trinity. This impressive building with a huge dome, left in ruins after the Second World War, was rebuilt not alone by the dedicated work of Polish Lutherans but also with help from many countries, especially the Lutheran World Federation. Seated at worship in that church, I was unable to understand the language but I felt comfortable with the liturgical order, which was stately. Even now as I look back I wish that I could effectively share with others the satisfaction I felt in the effectiveness of global cooperation in our church.

Although I now live in retirement, my wife and I decided that a vacation would be good. It should be said, however, that the motivation was primarily the bonus airline tickets whose time limits were about to expire. Choosing to visit Washington, D.C., our focus was primarily on the many museums of the Smithsonian. One could hardly leave these marvelous places without the sense that we are connected one to another, whether our interests are in natural history, technology, industry, air and space, or political and social history.

Our hotel was located within walking distance of the Washington Mall where one is imbued with a sense of history seeing the capitol building in one direction and the Washington Monument in the other. Walking from the hotel in the other direction, at Thomas Square we saw a statue of Martin Luther in front of Luther Place Church, a congregation known for its community and social activism.[1] Another church I noticed was St. John's Episcopal Church, a very simple and beautifully maintained old structure with a distinguished record. The sign board announced that it also had Spanish services so I entered and picked up some informational folders.

An additional taste of history was a side trip to Williamsburg, Virginia, a historic town restored and maintained by a Rockefeller

---

[1] This statue of Martin Luther is said to be the only full-size statue of Luther in the United States. It is a copy of the statue at Worms, Germany.

trust.[2] In addition to 88 original structures which have been preserved and restored, there have been several hundred reconstructions to the original specifications. Our lodging was in the Red Brick Tavern (no vittles or liquid refreshments) located on the Duke of Gloucester Street, not far from the Raleigh Tavern where the seeds of revolution grew. George Washington, Patrick Henry, Thomas Jefferson and James Madison were among those who met regularly at this place. It felt good to be connected to these people who were regarded by some as rebels. Was Thomas Paine really a scandalous firebrand on the edge of sedition and treason?

Inspired by the bonus travel tickets, we added to the trip a visit to Iceland—after all, only a hop, skip and jump away. [3] Much could be said about this delightful visit, but for the moment I'll mention the Hallgrimskirkja Church, which towers over the entire city of Reykjavik.[4] It's an amazing structure in both size and grace. Sandra and I took an elevator up to the 8th floor level in the church tower where the view was magnificent but we decided not to climb the additional stairs to the top. There are three large bells in the tower, each with a name, plus a carillon of 29 bells. Also amazing is the organ, which has 72 stops, 5,275 pipes and weighs some 25 tons. We talked for awhile with a student and later heard the organ as he and his teacher had a session together. Obviously he was an advanced student. Iceland is over 90% Lutheran but our visit at Hallgrimskirkja was not on a Sunday so I did not see whether the 1200 seats were filled.

Whether in Iceland or Poland it is clear that we are all strengthened by our ties with Lutherans around the world. In Christian discipleship there is no place for a private faith. Faith should be personal but not private. We are not to be "loner Christians". Instead, we should be giving thanks for the world-wide organization

---

[2] Instead of renting a car, as suggested by the travel agent, we chose to take the railroad to Williamsburg. It was a pleasant ride, free of the cares of driving in a strange area, let alone the stress and discomfort of airline travel. Our taxes pay for freeways and we subsidize the airlines. Why not build up a national rail system?

[3] Just three hours before our airliner's departure from Iceland Sandra tripped on the sidewalk. At first we thought it was a bad sprain but after hobbling and wheel chairs it turned out to be a fractured fibula above the ankle.

[4] The church is named after the Rev. Hallgrimur Pétursson (d 1674), "without doubt Iceland's most beloved poet. Iceland adopted Christianity in the year 1000 [and during] the Reformation in the16th century...became Lutheran. To this day over 90% of the Icelandic population belongs to the Lutheran Church". –Informational leaflet.

of the church, as in the Lutheran World Federation, gratefully recognizing the organizational instruments by which we express our faith.

33

The Trials of Democracy

December 21, 2002

The day after the elections I felt like wearing a black armband. But on second thought it is apparent that the Democrats deserved to lose because they were not standing for anything other than a hesitant opposition to the Republicans. Against an organized, determined and relentless party the Democrats had no backbone and could hardly merit the label of a loyal opposition.

The fact that I have not recently written any of these pages of comments and quotes has given rise to suggestions that the swing of political power to the so-called conservative wing has caused me to be discouraged or dispirited. I do wonder, as in the common statement that an alcoholic does not face reality until he is in the gutter, how long will it take the American public to recognize the harmful results of this administration's directions? Nevertheless I do retain an element of optimism. Perhaps my laxity in writing is due in part to a relaxing of my schedule in that recent issues of these Musings are not included in St. James' newsletters. In this time of transition following Pastor Smith's retirement I have chosen not to contribute these pages, which might be considered controversial.

We can be grateful for the Trent Lott scandal, not as a matter of partisan gloating but, as noted by one columnist, that it has opened the attic door to reveal secrets of Republican strength. The race issue, previously hidden by code words is now exposed. The solid Democratic South rapidly turned Republican in a trend beginning with Harry Truman's emphasis on civil rights. Recall the desegregation in the armed forces and the unwillingness of black veterans who had fought for freedom to accept segregation. In the 1960s Lyndon Johnson's remarkable legislative feats gave strength to the civil rights movement. Under Nixon and J. Edgar Hoover "law and order" was added to the list of code words and under the banner of "state's rights" white voters in southern states became Republican. How strange that state's rights are not important in many of the issues promoted by the right wing today. Until Trent Lott opened the door, there was the appearance that the old Confederacy had won after all—in that U.S. political leadership (and the religious right) is from the South.

Nevertheless there is a basis for optimism, as reflected by columnist Thomas Friedman:

When the Bush folks sneer at things like the World Court or Kyoto, and virtually every other treaty—without offering any alternatives but their own righteous power—"they project an arrogance and obsession with power alone," said the political theorist Yaron Erzahi.

> While other nations make fun of or scoff at America's naïve optimism, deep down they envy that optimism and rue the day we would give it up and adopt the tragic European view of history... It is also a huge source of U.S. strength and appeal—the soft power that comes from technologies, universities, Disney Worlds, movies and a Declaration of Independence built on the assumption that the future can bury the past. [1]

Friedman added that "the bin Ladenites know something Bush doesn't: that it is American optimism and soft power—not American hard power—that really threatens them".

Although President Bush's power and control are evident in almost every other headline and his managers have reduced the source material for comedians, there is a basis for optimism from another point of view, admittedly partisan. According to a book review, the authors of a recently published book state that

> the Bush administration is a flash in the pan, and the Democratic Party is becoming the new natural party of American government. Combining state-by-state analyses with a look at broader demographic trends (the growing importance of minority voters, the persistent failure of Republicans to appeal to upwardly mobile women, the widespread public suspicion of the religious right), *The Emerging Democratic Majority* is one of the most impressive overviews of American politics in recent years. [2]

---

[1] Thomas Friedman, "Preserving American Optimism," New York Times News Service, *The Oregonian*, Nov. 6, 2002.

[2] Walter Russell Mead, book review on *The Emerging Democratic Majority* by John B. Judis and Ruy Teixeira (New York: Scribner's, 2002), *Foreign Affairs* 81:6 (Nov/Dec 2002), p. 191.

The Trials of Democracy

Whether or not there is validity to the claim that this administration is "a flash in the pan," the Trent Lott scandal has damaged the view that adding control of Congress and the Supreme Court their party was leading to a new era of Republicanism. American flags, somewhat faded, are still plastered on car windows and bumpers (desecration of the flag?) and the President enjoys popularity as Commander in Chief—one reason for expanding the war against terrorism. [3] But how long can the patriotic fervor for war last? How long will the smooth words of the speech writers cover the unpopular actions of this party, as in tax cuts for the wealthy, rejection of environmental protection, the lack of health care for increasing numbers of people, etc.

Additional criticism is invited by the transparent alliance of top government leaders with corporate business, especially the oil business. One critic, Benjamin Barber, a professor of political philosophy, has written that private interests have weakened public life, reducing our trust in democratic institutions. [4] Pointing to corrupt business practices, he stated that they result from

> a failure of the instruments of democracy, which have been weakened by three decades of market fundamentalism, privatization ideology and resentment of government...[adding that] we have grown too timid as citizens, acquiescing to deregulation and privatization (airlines, accounting firms, banks, media conglomerates, you name it) and a growing tyranny of money over politics.
>
> The United States fails to see that the international treaties it won't sign, the criminal court it will not acknowledge and the United Nations system it does not adequately support are all efforts...at developing a new global contract to contain the chaos. The American belittlement of these efforts betrays a strategy that enhances global anarchy...
>
> The ascendant market ideology [as from the era of Reagan and Thatcher] claims to free us, but it actually robs us of the civic freedom by which we control the social consequences of our private choices.

---

[3] One critic has said that we are attempting to install democracy by force in Afghanistan and Iraq but are curtailing freedom in our own country (detention without charges, profiling of people, requiring libraries to tell what books one has read).

[4] Benjamin R. Barber, "A Failure of Democracy, not Capitalism," *The New York Times*, July 29, 2002. Barber teaches at the University of Maryland and is the author of *Jihad vs. McWorld*. The following quotation is from this source.

It was also noted by Barber that in the calamity of September 11 no one looked to Bill Gates, Kenneth Lay or Martha Stewart for leadership. People suddenly found new meaning in citizenship, public service and such occupations as fire-fighters and mayors. Patriotism calls for more than war-time flag waving and "support our troops" slogans. It calls for a broadening of vision and for courage to face the entrenched power of special interests. There is certainly opportunity for positive programs to counteract the Republican mantra of tax cut, tax cut, tax cut. For example, the Democratic governor of Vermont, Howard Dean proposed a repeal of the tax cut for the rich, suggesting universal health coverage in its place. President Bush, however, appears to have his heart set on making the rich richer and invading Iraq under his doctrine of preemption. [5]

---

[5] Speaking of preemption, "The Bush administration announced today it will seek congressional approval and United Nations backing for a pre-emptive attack on Norway. Defense Secretary Donald Rumsfeld told reporters the CIA has learned that Norway has been stockpiling a weapon of mass destruction, a mysterious substance called 'lutefisk'" (Source unknown).

34

Foreboding in Issues Foreign and Domestic

March 15, 2003

Leaving the front door with a newspaper, I responded to a pleasant greeting from a neighbor but while waiting for the elevator her face reflected anger as she read the headline. Ordering coffee at the deli the manager's cheerful greeting turned to a suppressed anger with reference to the headline. In both cases there was more than a tinge of sadness; there was dismay at the direction in which the Bush administration is leading our country. The apprehension which appears just under the surface of normalcy is not simply about a war against Iraq, although that is clearly the focus. It was September 11 which, dreadful in itself, was the key which unlocked Pandora's box, giving a shaky president sudden credibility and uniting a nation eager to follow his confident, albeit swaggering, leadership. We had the support and friendship of the whole world in the struggle against terrorism. But the struggle against the perpetrators of 9/11 turned into a war and the war became open ended, sliding into a preemptive war not related to 9/11 and a foreign policy divergent from our heritage. Moreover, under the guise of national security, a term used frequently by dictators in Latin America and Germany, we are losing the America we desire to safeguard, causing many of us to be uneasy, even fearful, in anticipating the future.

Friends have asked why my writing of these pages has become infrequent and I can only guess at the answer: that I have been overwhelmed by the several stacks of news clippings, reprints from my printer, and notes from journals—a challenge for this amateur social critic. Years before I retired I wrote such pages as these, which I called commentaries, and mailed them to family and friends. They were means by which I reflected on current readings. As a means of expression they were often expansions of letters I would write to political figures. Some of the themes would deal directly with religion but more often than not the commentary themes would reflect the social responsibility implicit in the Christian faith. It has long been my practice to clip newspaper items and write notes on readings in various journals. I don't have the ability or the resources to make striking contributions to the mass of printed matter flooding us. However, I write to express myself, a self-satisfying additional step to casting a vote in the ballot box.

Foreign Policy

Bush is not the first American president seeking a regime change in Iraq; other presidents for nearly half a century have been using the CIA as the agent for changes of leadership and coups, according to historian Roger Morris. [1] He writes that American interventions are well known in the Middle East and in Europe and for this reason U.S. policy is viewed with cynicism. [2] Since the coups have been followed by bloody reprisals, Morris concluded with this thought: "If a new war in Iraq seems fraught with danger and uncertainty, just wait for the peace".

There is no doubt that a regime change in Iraq would be desirable, although there is no clarity on the alternative. Even among Islamic people there are few who would defend Saddam Hussein. But the question is whether an American invasion is the best course of action. With strong support in the United Nations a credible case

---

[1] Roger Morris, "A Tyrant 40 Years in the Making," *New York Times* March 14, 2003. Morris is author of *Richard Milhous Nixon: The Rise of an American Politician*.

[2] Some abbreviated excerpts from "A Tyrant 40 Years in the Making" illustrate this history, as follows: 40 years ago the CIA conducted its own regime change in Baghdad. The Iraqi leader seen as a grave threat in 1963 was Abdel Karim Kassem, a general who five years earlier had deposed the Western-allied Iraqi monarchy. Washington had a role in the coup.

From 1958 to 1960, despite Kassem's harsh repression, the Eisenhower administration abided him as a counter to Washington's nemesis of the era, Gamal Abdel Nasser of Egypt—much as Ronald Reagan and George H.W. Bush would aid Saddam Hussein in the 1980s against the common foe of Iran.

In 1958 infighting among the new leaders brought another coup in which Baathist general Ahmed Hassan al-Bakr seized control, bringing to the threshold of power his kinsman, Saddam Hussein—all this with the CIA's backing.

In 1963 Britain and Israel backed American intervention in Iraq, while other U.S. allies—chiefly France and Germany—resisted. American agents marshaled opponents of the Iraqi regime under the CIA's "Health Alteration Committee." On Feb. 8, 1963, the conspirators staged a coup in Baghdad. Eventually Kassem gave up and after a swift trial was shot. A bloodbath followed using CIA lists of suspected Communists and leftists.

As its instrument the CIA had chosen the authoritarian and anti-Communist Baath Party. The U.S. sent arms to the new regime, weapons later used against the same Kurdish insurgents the U.S. had backed against Kassem and then abandoned. Soon, Western corporations like Mobil, Bechtel and British Petroleum were doing business with Baghdad.

might be made for military action but not otherwise. The president has often been criticized for not presenting effective arguments for an attack. Reasons given have often been generalized and occasionally withdrawn, such as Iraqi links with bin Laden. The worldwide good will toward America after September 11 has been squandered by an apparent arrogance which strangely denigrates the United Nations, trashes the Kyoto global warming treaty, tells the Russians we are scrapping the ABM treaty, and scorns environmental protection. Now that friendly nations would be helpful we read about bribes which mount to the billions of dollars. Columnist Maureen Dowd wrote that "It will go down as a great mystery of history how Mr. Popularity at Yale metamorphosed into President Persona Non Grata of the world... Just when you thought it couldn't get more Strangelovian it does".

Presenting the case against a military attack on Iraq, Robert Kuttner, editor of *The American Prospect*, wrote that the critics are the realists and the "Cheney-Rumsfeld-Wolfowitz contingent the naïve idealists". Referring to the cold war's Stalin, Khrushchev and Brezhnev, who made Saddam Hussein "look minor league," he wrote that

> the spiritual ancestors of Cheney et al. taunted the Truman administration as "Dean Acheson's Cowardly College of Communist Containment," [although] the Kennan-Acheson strategy of hemming in Stalin rather than starting World War III was the right policy. President Eisenhower overruled ultra-hawks who wanted preemptive nuclear war... There was fierce lobbying urging intervention when Khruschchev brutally put down the Hungarian revolution of 1956, and again in the Czech spring of 1968. But wiser heads grasped that the Soviets considered Eastern Europe a sphere of influence... By being both tough and patient, we have seen one totalitarian regime after another fall. [3]

Kuttner added that an attack on Iraq would not directly risk nuclear war but it would include other risks, e.g. "fracturing NATO, wrecking the United Nations, legitimatizing preemptive strikes, attracting more converts to Islamist fanaticism and warping America's conception of our own vital interests".

---

[3] Robert Kuttner, "Radicals in Power," *The American Prospect*, March 2003, p. 3.

Domestic Concerns Neglected

Recognizing that there has been very little debate on the steady erosion of civil liberties, almost hidden under the cover of "national security," a well known author, Wendell Berry, wrote an essay which appeared on a full page of *The New York Times*, entitled "A Citizen's Response to the National Security Strategy of the United States of America. [4] Following are excerpts from Berry's essay:

> The New National Security Strategy published by the White House in September 2002, if carried out, would amount to a radical revision of the political character of our nation. Its central and most significant statement is this:
>
>> While the United States will constantly strive to enlist the support of the international community, we will not hesitate to act alone, if necessary, to exercise our right of self-defense by acting preemptively against such terrorists.
>
> A democratic citizen must deal here first of all with the question, Who is this "we"? It is not the "we" of the Declaration of Independence ... [or] of the Constitution... This "we" of the new strategy can refer only to the president. It is a royal "we"... The alleged justification for this new strategy is the recent emergence in the United States of international terrorism. But why the events of September 11, 2001, horrifying as they were, should have called for a radical new investiture of power in the executive branch is not clear... The war against terrorism is not, strictly speaking, a war against nations. This is a war against "the embittered few"...
>
> Much of the obscurity of our effort so far against terrorism originates in the now official idea that the enemy is evil and that we are (therefore) good, which is the precise mirror image of the official idea of the terrorists. The epigraph of Part III of The National Security Strategy contains this sentence from President Bush's speech at the National Cathedral on September 14, 2001: "But our responsibility to history is already clear: to answer these attacks and rid the world of evil." A government committing its nation to rid the world of evil, is assuming necessarily that it and its nation are good...
>
> And so it is not without reason or precedent that a citizen should point out that, in addition to evils originating abroad and supposedly correctable by catastrophic technologies in "legitimate" hands, we have an agenda of domestic evils, not only those that properly self-

---

[4] Wendell Berry, "A Citizen's Response...", *The New York Times*, Feb. 2, 2003, p. 5. The essay was sponsored by the Orion Society (www.oriononline.org). Berry is the author of more than thirty books, including *In the Presence of Fear: Three Essays for a Changed World*.

aware humans can find in their own hearts, but also several that are indigenous to our history as a nation: issues of economic and social justice, and issues related to the continuing and worsening maladjustment between our economy and our land.

It is quite clear that these domestic evils are being ignored, bypassed for another cause. Columnist Georgie Ann Geyer, quoting a feature article in Newsweek, wrote that the Bush administration appears to be on a "messianic mission" and his intention of invading Iraq is "based primarily on religious obsession and visions of personal grandiosity". Geyer again quoted the article in saying that the White House reflects a "sense of destiny that approaches the Calvinistic" with no attention given to the classic Christian views on a "just war".[5] This linkage with religion has also been explored by Régis DeBray, an author and a former adviser to President Francois Mitterrand of France, who wrote:

> The United States, of course, is free to decide that a cadaverous satrap, kept under close surveillance, affects its national (and familial) interests. If the American administration is intent on precipitating the war, that is Osama bin Laden's fondest wish, if it wants to give fundamentalism, which is currently ebbing, a second chance, we can only say, so much the worse for you—while regretting that history's most constant law, the perverse effect, is not better known to the Pentagon. Provoking chaos in the name of order, and resentment instead of gratitude, is something to which all empires are accustomed.
>
> The stakes are spiritual. Europe defends a secular vision of the world. It does not separate matters of urgency from long-term considerations. The United States compensates for its shortsightedness, its tendency to improvise, with an altogether biblical self-assurance in its transcendent destiny. Puritan America is hostage to a sacred morality; it regards itself as the predestined repository of Good, with a mission to strike down Evil. Trusting in Providence, it pursues a politics that is at bottom theological and as old as Pope Gregory VII.[6]

With or without religious motivation, it is evident that the all-consuming drive to attack Iraq has meant that scant attention has been given to serious domestic problems. From across the Atlantic, John le Carré, wrote that

---

[5] Georgie Ann Geyer, "War and Religion," Universal Press Syndicate, *The Oregonian*, March 7, 2003.

> America has entered one of its periods of historical madness, but this is the worst I can remember: worse than McCarthyism, worse than the Bay of Pigs and in the long term potentially more disastrous than the Vietnam War. As in McCarthy times, the freedoms that have made America the envy of the world are being systematically eroded. The combination of compliant US media and vested corporate interests is once more ensuring that a debate which should be ringing out in every town square is confided to the loftier columns of the East Coast press… Last Friday a friend of mine in California drove to his local supermarket with a sticker on his car saying: "Peace is also Patriotic". It was gone by the time he'd finished shopping. [7]

President Bush exudes confidence in his posture, in his elbows-out macho walk and in his simplistic statements explaining his mission to "rid the world of evil," thus pleasing his religious friends of the right wing as well as his secular hawks. [8] Standing in contrast are words of Régis deBray, mentioned above:

> Europe no longer possesses that euphoric arrogance. It is done mourning the Absolute and conducts its politics…politically. It is past the age of ultimatums, protectorates at the other end of the planet, and the white man's burden. Is that the age America is entering?

There is a positive note to mention in the context of the Middle East. A friend and neighbor who is now the interim president of the American University in Cairo, Egypt, has mentioned the high regard in which American education is held in that part of the world. A comparable school is in Lebanon and others are being established in Jordan, Azerbaijan, Kazakhstan, Morocco and other countries. Thus when I noticed an article by John Waterbury, president of the American University in Beirut, "Hate Your Policies, Love Your Institutions," I read it carefully. [9] He wrote that

---

[6] Régis deBray, "The French Lesson," *New York Times*, Feb. 23, 2003

[7] John leCarré, "The United States of America has gone mad," *The Times*, United Kingdom, Jan. 15, 2003

[8] The image of Don Quixote came to mind but was instantly rejected because there is no humor in the direction this administration is taking. With a focus on Iraq almost no attention is given to the serious manipulations of Attorney General Ashcroft.

America is admired for its transparent politics, independent judiciary, adherence to due process, encouragement of entrepreneurship, linking of rewards to performance, provision of economic opportunity, and rapid social mobility. Perhaps no single institutional feature of American dominance is more admired than its system of higher education. Even radical Islamists are not shy about sending their children to be educated in the United States.

Waterbury noted that higher education cannot resolve "clashing interests or inimical policies" but it can have a strong influence in working through the conflicts. American education encourages the open debate of issues and the "cultivation of a skeptical attitude toward perceived wisdom". That attitude is clearly needed here in the United States, lest we lose the values we take for granted.

Post Script

These pages were written prior to the current headlines of an imminent invasion but the points made remain valid.

Although not related directly to the Iraqi issue, the Palestinians are significantly affected. Almost ignored by the media (where is that so-called liberal press?) one is forced to look elsewhere for news. [10] One source I respect is the Lutheran church's use of bulletins through the Internet, often quoting Lutheran Bishop Younan in Jerusalem. See MENET@LISTSERV.ELCA.ORG, an ELCA Mid-East networking list. It is particularly discouraging for me to read about the struggles of the Lutheran World Federation to maintain the Augusta Victoria Hospital on the Mount of Olives in its service primarily to Palestinians. To read about Israeli snipers in the hospital's towers or the barricades against ambulances is unsettling.

---

[9] John Waterbury, "Hate Your Policies, Love Your Institutions," *Foreign Affairs*, 82:1 (January/February 2003), pp. 58-68.

[10] One source of information is the "Legislative Update" produced by the Lutheran Office for Governmental Affairs, 122 C Street NW, Suite 125, Washington, DC 20001-2172. See: www.elca.org/dcs/studies.html. See also: Loga@elca.org or www.loga.org.

War and Consequences

April 23, 2003

The War on (in) Iraq

There was never any doubt as to who would win the war on (in) Iraq. Writers from the left and right both overstated their arguments. I am glad that I made no indefensible statements. I fully support the position taken by the ELCA's Presiding Bishop Mark S. Hanson on March 20 in which he expressed his "profound concern that the United States has chosen to take the step of a preemptive strike," stating that our country, "especially because of its wealth and might, has a particular responsibility to pursue policies of cooperation and to seek to resolve conflicts peacefully". He added that we must "reclaim for ourselves any language of faith that has been used to wage war and ensure that it is used for the sake of peace and reconciliation". [1]

News reports have given glowing reports about the small number of American casualties but I have not yet seen even an estimate of Iraqi deaths and injuries. There is no question that Saddam Hussein was an evil man who inflicted death, pain and suffering to many people but the question remains as to how much death, pain and suffering has been caused by his removal. Moreover, there should be recognition of the suffering caused by the destruction of the infrastructure and the economy.

The Consequences

We speak of the war in the past tense and it is true that heavy warfare is over but what about the consequences? If the aim beyond the removal of the dictator and the removal of weapons of mass destruction (which have not yet been discovered) is truly to be the installation of democracy, the challenge is enormous. The United States has been involved in the rebuilding of Germany and Japan and in drawing Eastern Europe, including Russia, into the western family.

---

[1] Statement by the Rev. Mark S. Hanson, Presiding Bishop, Evangelical Lutheran Church in America, March 20, 2003.

War and Consequences

However, Heinrich Winkler, a professor of modern history in Berlin, worries about the lack of post-war planning in the conservative think tanks. He stated that in 1918 Mesopotamia [Iraq] had just then been "cobbled together out of three former provinces of the defunct Ottoman Empire" but that two years later "Iraq was in the midst of a bloody Shiite rebellion against British rule". The basic differences, ethnic, religious and political, evident in those provinces continue to exist. [2]

> Lingering in his mind, Mr. Winkler said, is the recent example of Algeria, which did become a sort of democracy, one in which a fundamentalist Islamic party won the first ever free elections, an event that led to bloody civil strife. If democracy came to Iraq, a country without the moderate civic culture that genuine democracy requires, the Shiites would find themselves in a majority, and the result could well be an anti-American theocracy.

The challenge of establishing a stable democratic nation is not simply a matter of bringing together diverse elements within its borders but also reaches into the region. The border with Iran in recent years was the scene of a bitter war and children who died as martyrs have not been forgotten. Next door is Turkey, wary of its large number of Kurdish people, who together with the Kurds of northern Iraq and adjacent Iran are a sizeable number.

Another complicating regional factor is the tremendous anger toward America evident among Islamic people, deepened because of U. S. support of Israel and its determined oppression of Palestinians. Although President Bush is a nominal Methodist, he appears to be "closer to evangelical and fundamentalist beliefs and sensibilities, which are increasingly evident in his...conception of Saddam as a member of the axis of evil," as noted by the author Kevin Phillips. [3] He also stated that "No one has ever asked George W. whether he believes in Armageddon, but U.S. troops are now moving along the Euphrates River, the biblical border of the land of Israel". This is an important factor in the support of Israel by Christian conservatives who believe that Israel must be re-established as a

---

[2] Richard Bernstein, "Hyper Power," *The New York Times,* March 23, 2003.
[3] Kevin Phillips, "The father, son and 'footsteps factor' eerily build to war in Iraq," The Oregonian, April 6, 2003. Phillips is the author of *Wealth and Democracy: A Political History of the American Rich* and other books of political commentary.

necessary step toward Armageddon and the millenial rule of Christ.[4] Phillips wonders what long-term consequences there might be from Bush's religious leanings.

In describing the neighboring Iranian revolution, author Elizabeth Rubin has written that reformers favor a "go-slow approach to democracy" because they remember the problems caused by the regime change which occurred about 25 years ago.[5] She wrote:

> As for American designs to democratize the Middle East, the students are intrigued but wary. They are puzzled by Bush's religious and ideological rhetoric. "We're trying to move from ideology to modernity, and Bush is moving from modernity to ideology," one student leader told me.

Having squandered international good will after September 11 and having alienated traditionally friendly nations, the United States has also rejected the involvement of the United Nations in the rebuilding of Iraq, all in the interest of having total control or being sole masters. Recent news that the U.S. will permanently maintain five air bases in Iraq can only add to anti-American anger in the region. This is not welcome news to mid-eastern capitals, such as Damascus or Teheran. Moreover, the first two firms to have huge contracts for reconstruction in Iraq are Bechtel and Haliburton, both firms having close ties to the Bush inner circle. Will the British be allowed to bid on any projects in what has been called the Iraqi "money tree"? Will Iraqi people have anything to say about their oil?

A price must be paid for this venture and although the price encompasses more than money, finance is certainly a significant factor. War-like terms are used by Jeff Madrick, writing on "The Iraqi Time Bomb" as follows:

> Mix the open-ended costs of war and reconstruction with huge tax cuts, shrinking tax revenues and a stalled economy, and you get a budget deficit bound to explode. The victims will be many... The denial of economic reality that permeated Wall Street a few years ago has now migrated to Washington... Here are some of the facts. Even without a war, the budget deficit would have exceeded $300

---

[4] Strange as this may sound, a few decades ago some Christian conservatives claimed that God's cause in Armageddon could be aided by nuclear means, thus advancing the date of Armageddon.

[5] Elizabeth Rubin, "The Millimeter Revolution," *New York Times Magazine,* Aril 6, 2003, pp. 38-43.

billion this year—just three years after the budget experienced a surplus of nearly $240 billion. (This was in the midst of a four-year run of substantial surpluses.) But with war costs escalating and revenues falling as a result of the flat economy, this year's deficit could rise to $400 billion. In fiscal year 2004, it is likely to be higher. [6]

Far be it from me to make any critical comments on the economic turf; I have no credibility in what is known as the "dismal science". However, I can quote credible writers who use figures close to those above, who say that the risk of another recession is real, who report that the U.S. lost 108,000 jobs in March on top of a loss of 357,000 jobs in February. In personal experience I immediately think of several well qualified people who have been out of work for over a year. How many teachers might have been employed for the price of one smart bomb? Multiply that figure for third-world salaries. Could basic health coverage have been provided for the 41 million Americans currently without insurance for the price of the bombs, missiles and rockets rained on Iraq? (Was Bill Clinton brave or naïve in proposing universal coverage?), A one-time presidential candidate, George McGovern, has some hard-hitting comments:

> Thanks to the most crudely partisan decision in the history of the Supreme Court, the nation has been given a President of painfully limited wisdom and compassion and lacking any sense of the nation's true greatness. Appearing to enjoy his role as Commander in Chief of the armed forces above all other functions of his office, and unchecked by a seemingly timid Congress, a compliant Supreme court, a largely subservient press and a corrupt corporate plutocracy, George W. Bush has set the nation on a course for one-man rule.
> He treads carelessly on the Bill of Rights, the United Nations and international law while creating a costly but largely useless new federal bureaucracy loosely called "Homeland Security". Meanwhile, such fundamental building blocks of national security as full employment and a strong labor movement are of no concern. The nearly $1.5 trillion tax giveaway, largely for the further enrichment of those already rich, will have to be made up by cutting government services and shifting a larger share of the tax burden to workers and the elderly. This President and his advisers know well how to get us involved in imperial crusades abroad while pillaging the ordinary American at home. The same families who are exploited by a rich man's government find their sons and daughters being called to war,

---

[6] Jeff Madrick, "The Iraqi Time Bomb," *New York Times Magazine*, April 6, 2003, pp. 46-51.

as they were in Vietnam—but not the sons of the rich and well connected...

Following the 9/11 tragedy at the World Trade Center and the Pentagon, the entire world was united in sympathy and support for America. But thanks to the arrogant unilateralism, the bullying and the clumsy, unimaginative diplomacy of Washington, Bush converted a world of support into a world united against us, with the exception of Tony Blair and one or two others... [7]

How one wishes for an America standing as a beacon of light, reflecting hope, having positive goals! Instead of the Statue of Liberty we have harsh immigration officials (*la migra*, to Latin Americans) and international airports are full of unsmiling officials, camouflage suits and machine guns. The White House is locked in secrecy as historical records (e.g. Reagans' records) are sealed from the public. Individual privacy is threatened as Homeland Security, enabled by technology, is developing profile banks. In criminal "justice" detainees are held indefinitely. McGovern's thought concerning one-man rule is frightening.

Roger Williams

My mother-in-law likes to claim Roger Williams as one of her ancestors, so I must tell her that his birthday is this year but that she need not send him a card. The exact date is not known but it was probably in the year 1603, making this the 400th anniversary. In 1984 the U.S. National Park Service created the Roger Williams National Memorial in Providence, Rhode Island, and on May 10 and 11 there will be special events in honor of the 400th anniversary of Roger Williams' birth. In a descriptive account Rob Boston wrote the following:

> In 1635 Roger Williams was appointed to pastoral duties at the local church in Salem, Mass. Williams, a puritan preacher who had fled religious persecution in England, was already unpopular in Boston for rebuking authorities who seized lands owned by Native Americans...[Moreover] Massachusetts' General Court required...an oath of allegiance to the King of England, ending with "so help me, God". Most people did not see a problem with that. Williams did. To

---

[7] George McGovern, "The Reason Why," *The Nation*, April 21, 2003.

him, the state's use of God's name in a civil oath was far from innocuous. What about the atheists, he argued? [8]

His position that civil authorities should have no authority in religious matters irked the authorities, who ordered him to leave their jurisdiction. In his own time he did leave and purchased a plot of land from the Indians. With his wife and children he established a new settlement which he called Providence. Boston quoted the historian Edwin Gaustad, writing: "Although Rhode Island prospered slowly, it hung on to become the safest refuge for liberty of conscience. Dissenters of all stripes, persons of all religious persuasions or none, could find sanctuary in Rhode Island".

Although Roger Williams was blunt and direct, lacking in grace, he was ahead of his time as he argued for the separation of state and church, long before the influence of James Madison and Thomas Jefferson. That Williams was certainly controversial was noted by Boston, who wrote that President John Quincy Adams called Williams "a polemical porcupine" whose refusal to swear the oath of the Court was "seditious".

The concept of the separation of church and state is before us again as the Bush administration tries to break down that "wall" of separation in areas of education and social action. President Reagan also tried to cross that line or wall in matters of welfare—perhaps to shift responsibility to the churches thus to lessen taxes (and concern). Back in the 1950s the Rev. Franklin Clark Fry, president of the United Lutheran Church in America, publicized the phrase "institutional separation and functional interaction".

Recognizing that the religious right wing is eager to make use of the power of the state and its money, it is strange to read that TV preacher Pat Robertson is calling for the United States to establish a secular state with complete separation of church and state in post-war Iraq. Barry Lynn, the director of Americans United for Separation of Church and State, pointed out that Robertson's argument was that in an open vote a "Shi'ite majority would prevail and...without separation...all the other religious and ethnic groups could suffer: the Sunni Muslims, the orthodox Christians, the Assyrian Christians and the Kurds for starters". [9] That is exactly the case for

---

[8] Rob Boston, "The Forgotten Founder," *Church and State,* April 2003, published by Americans United for the Separation of Church and State.

[9] Barry W. Lynn, "Pat and Separation: An Amazing Conversion by Reverend Robertson?" *Church and State,* April 2003.

the separation but Robertson does not apply it to the United States. According to Lynn, Robertson works with President Bush, frequently claiming that he helped elect him and wants the power of government to enact the "Bible-based morality that Robertson touts daily on his television show". The strange turnabout, as Lynn wrote, is that Robertson has on several occasions "asserted that church-state separation is a communist, Soviet-style doctrine." Lynn noted that just last year at a Christian Coalition conference in Washington, Robertson called separation a "distortion" and a "lie foisted on us".

Resources

Regarding the Palestinians, Christians in Palestine, messages from the Rev. Munib Younan, Bishop of the Evangelical Lutheran Church in Jerusalem, the (Lutheran) Augusta Victoria Hospital on the Mount of Olives, and others: ELCA Mid-East Networking List: MENET@LISTSERV.ELCA.ORG
    For further information: Ann Hafften (ELCA): annhafften@MINDSPRING.COM
    Also: www.holyland-lutherans.org/amman
    www.elca.org/middleeast
    www.loga.org (Lutheran office for governmental affairs)
Another resource is Friends of Sabeel—North America, an ecumenical group supporting Palestinian churches but wanting a just peace for both Palestine and Israel, led by the Rev. Canon Richard Toll, an Episcopal priest in Milwaukie, Oregon. See: www.Sabeel.org

A Billion

A billion is a difficult number to comprehend, but one advertising agency did a good job of putting that figure into perspective in one of its releases:
    A billion seconds ago it was 1959.
    A billion minutes ago Jesus was alive
    A billion hours ago our ancestors were living in
        the Stone Age.
    A billion dollars ago was only 8 hours and 20 minutes,
        at the rate Washington spends it.
                —source unknown

A Century of Flight

November 22, 2003

Dec. 17 marks a century of flight

There will be a great celebration on December 17 at the Wright Brothers National Memorial, Kill Devil Hills, North Carolina, marking a century since that first flight. A replica of the Wright Flyer, a faithful version of the original built by the Experimental Aircraft Association (EAA—rhymes with Oshkosh), is expected to be flown twice at the First Flight Airport on December 17.

A mechanic-friend, David Domeyer, told me emphatically that every airplane with an airworthy certificate should be in the air on that day. I sincerely hope that my Navion N4799K will be out of the shop prior to that date but since I'll be out of town at that time I'll find someone to celebrate the day by flying it. [1]

Richard Collins, an editor of Flying magazine, wrote that he had been "flying solo for 52 percent of the history of powered flight". [2] Pausing a moment, it occurred to me that I could say the same. Having learned how to fly in 1951, I can also claim 52% of the century of flight. A year or so later I joined AOPA and now my lapel wings have a 50-year bar. [3] In his article Collins noted some of the remarkable changes in the last half century. When he (and I) started flying in

---

[1] A couple years ago I sold my 1946 Stinson and, wanting something more modern, bought a 1949 Navion (North American *avion*), a model which has been a life-long dream. My mechanic-friend and I examined the plane and I decided to buy it. However, it soon became clear that we were not told the whole truth, to state it most charitably. The log books had false entries. Moreover, the problems were not all discovered at once. One thing after another needed correction. So now, after a year and a half, I continue to look forward to a first flight—any day now.

[2] Richard L. Collins, "Over Half a Century of Flight," *Flying*, December 2003, p. 17.

[3] Aircraft Owners and Pilots Association (AOPA) and the Experimental Aircraft Association (EAA) are two major organizations which support general aviation (as distinct from the airlines and military). The word "experimental" does not refer to daredevil innovation but is an official category of aircraft which are not "store-bought" or produced under regulated circumstances for U.S. civilian use.

1951 in J-3 Cubs, which were our trainers, they could be purchased for $750. Back in the late 1950s a beautiful Navion on the field caught my eye and it became my life-long dream. Its price was $5,000 but the dream was put on hold because my annual salary was $3,000. Collins wrote that in those days the "ultimate business airplanes were Bonanzas, Navions and Cessna 195s". He went on to say:

> The "romance" that used to be associated with flying started dissipating after World War I and was fully gone a while back... Flying is a challenge in a society that has become risk averse, almost to the point of paranoia... There will be great developments in the future, but a lot of elements will stay about the same for a long time. In the first 100 years of civil aviation we went from a few knots to a Mach 2 airliner. Who knows whether we'll see a similar acceleration in the next 100 years.

The Wright Vin Fiz (the name of a popular drink) made the first flight across the United States in 1911, from Sheepshead Bay, N.Y., to Pasadena. The pilot, Calbraith Perry Rodgers, had learned to fly with Orville and Wilbur and then flew the 4,321 miles, followed (or led) by three support cars, one of which carried parts needed for frequent repairs, necessary because the plane and pilot survived 70 landings and 12 crashes.

In contrast to the Vin Fiz, my Navion in its early days has flown to Alaska, to Acapulco and to Havana, Cuba. Of course, back then radios were not necessities and this particular Navion was then in good condition with authentic innards. But now that the mechanic, André Krivitsky, is about to release the plane from his shop as legal to fly, I'll have to persuade the current occupant of the White House to open up relations with Cuba. One little story should be told: I bought this airplane from an Idaho farmer and it had no radios in it except for a CB, which he used to talk to other farmers and truckers! The airplane has now sprouted seven antennae, installed with their significant boxes. As you may have recognized, I have been keenly interested in aviation but, alas! my budgets have been limited. To illustrate, my funds are slightly lacking for the $20 million needed for the privatized space experience with the Russians. If I were invited to visit the space station, I would instantly accept. I should have been a corporate executive in a de-regulated and privatized business. [4]

---

[4] Hefty contributions to the Vice President might be helpful.

On to the next century

What remarkable feats will be accomplished in the second century of powered flight? Do we need another Kennedy to offer a vision comparable to sending a man to the moon and bringing him back? Or will it take a race (preferably economic) with the Chinese to set foot on Mars? Columbus set foot on a whole new world during the time of Luther but Europeans considered the overseas discoveries insignificant. They were far too preoccupied with the fear of the Turk and fighting their religious/economic wars to consider the enormous potential of the discoveries. Thinking of that landing on the moon, it is a pleasant memory to recall that the entire world admired and applauded the United States. But now—what a contrast! Descriptive key words for America are greed and narcissism, words which are apt for many an average voter, many of our corporations, and much of our foreign policy. I am now rejecting the temptation to use the analogy of the alcoholic's need to fall in the gutter before climbing out. That is far too risky. But consider the topics of discussion: jobs, education, global warming, health insurance, trade imbalance, national debt, militarism, civil rights, and even the decaying infrastructure, as well as the repudiation of international treaties. They all call for a vision which is sadly lacking. But where is the energy? Whose are the exuberant voices? Among the loudest are those on the Christian right wing of religion, eager for the power of the state to enforce views which would support a theocracy or appear very close to a civil religion. Is this actually the momentum? Unfortunately, a reactionary fundamentalism is also evident in other religions in other lands and the case has been made that our foreign policy is fomenting that drive, illustrated by the imperceptive comment "Bring them on".

My vision of a second century appears to have moved from aviation and space to other aspects of our times and I now see that I should close this section with a positive note, but frankly I'm at a loss. Any suggestions?

Unable to continue after writing the two paragraphs above, I slouched in a chair with a book purchased the other day at Powell's — Molly Ivins, *Bushwhacked*, which is almost a sequel to her earlier book, *Shrub*.[5] In the introduction she noted that the first book in 1999 was about the man's years as governor of Texas and then she wrote

---

[5] Molly Ivins and Lou Dubose, *Bushwhacked*, Random House, 2003. A couple weeks ago I heard her speak at the nearby Congregational Church. She had been invited by Powell's Books for a talk and a book-signing event, but there was such demand that larger accommodations were necessary. It was great fun to listen to her.

"We were tempted to begin this book by observing, 'If y'all had've read the first book, we wouldn't've had to write this one.' Cooler heads prevailed".

My spirits perked up with a few pages in her book. Dismissing the Washington press corps as "ever more courtierlike," she wrote in the introduction that she would start at the other end with "average citizens".

> The good news is that nothing will cheer you up more about this country than getting out and talking to the people in it. We were prepared to play a dirge on our literary violin for the hapless victims of various misbegotten and mean-spirited policies. Unfortunately for our purposes, we kept finding Americans who are tough, funny, sassy, brave, smart and full of fight... We found heroes all over hell and gone. Most of them are "ordinary people," some of them are government bureaucrats, and a few of them are even politicians.

Optimism has been revived.

An Unthinkable Thought

The radical thought is that Israel should "be replaced by a binational country in which Jews and Palestinians would live together". [6] In the *New York Times* Edward Rothstein wrote what appeared to be shocking statements. He was quoting the "distinguished historian" Tony Judt, who had previously in *The New York Review of Books* declared that "the time has come to think the unthinkable," that there is 'no place in the world today for a 'Jewish state'". In a later response to critics, according to Rothstein, Judt described American defenders of Israel as "useful idiots" and argued that they fail to see Zionism as "the dogma of intolerant, belligerent, self-righteous, God-fearing irredentists".

Although these thoughts are regarded by many as shocking, Judt cites respected names who share his thoughts. Among those mentioned are the playwright Joshua Sobol and the Israeli writer Amos Elon, who praised Judt for "cutting through a forest of clichés". Rothstein added:

> In August, in interviews in Haretz, two leftist Israelis, Meron Benvenisti and Haim Hanegbi, went even further in their expressions of disgust with Israel's sins and settlements. "A Jewish state can no

---

[6] Edward Rothstein, "Seeking an Alternative To a Jewish State" (Connections), *The New York Times*, Nov. 22, 2003.

longer exist here," Mr. Hanegbi says. Mr. Benvenisti, who has long argued about the baleful demographic consequences of holding onto the West Bank, sees a binational state as inevitable: "The Zionist revolution is over".

Rothstein noted that expressions of "self blame and binational impulse" are only partly the result of current problems. Quoting several studies on this aspect of Zionism, he wrote that although Theodor Herzl advocated Jewish sovereignty, others did not:

> [S]uch imposing figures as Martin Buber, Judah Magnes, Gershom Scholem and other German Jewish settlers in Palestine, in forming Brit Shalom in 1925, opposed Jewish political power, hoping at most for what Buber called a "binational social political entity" binding Arabs and Jews. [7]

Rothstein noted that the theologian Martin Buber accused the Jews of "mistakenly following the way of power, saying that the 'Jewish people preferred to learn from Hitler rather than from us,'" strong words said in 1958. The author also noted that Shimon Peres in his book *The New Middle East* (1993) "envisioned the end of all nation states, the weakening of religious identities and the rise of new regional allegiances".

Sensitive to the Anguished Debate

An excerpt from a reflection on Zionism by Israeli leader Avraham Burg was provided by Churches for Middle East Peace (CMEP) with this note: "Burg's article reminds us of the need to be sensitive to the...anguished debate within the American Jewish community". [8] The introduction to Burg's article stated that the writer, Avraham Burg is a "prominent Israeli whose father, Dr. Joseph Burg, was a leading religious and political figure in the early days of the State of Israel. It was published in the August 29 edition of the "Forward," a New York weekly Jewish newspaper (www.forward.com)".

---

[7] Mentioned were the following: Yoram Hazony, *The Jewish State: The Struggle for Israel's Soul* (Basic Books, 2000) and Arthur Hertzberg, *The Fate of Zionism* (Harper, San Francisco).

[8] This article was received from the ELCA Mid-East Networking List (MENET@LISTSERV.ELCA.ORG)

A Century of Flight

Forward
A failed Israeli society collapses while its leaders remain silent.

By Avraham Burg
Avraham Burg was speaker of Israel's Knesset from 1999 to 2003 and is a former chairman of the Jewish Agency for Israel. He is currently a Labor Party Knesset member. This essay is adapted by the author from an article that appeared in Yediot Aharonot.
August 29, 2003
    The Zionist revolution has always rested on two pillars; a just path and an ethical leadership. Neither of these is operative any longer. The Israeli nation today rests on a scaffolding of corruption, and on foundations of oppression and injustice. As such, the end of the Zionist enterprise is already on our doorstep. There is a real chance that ours will be the last Zionist generation. There may yet be a Jewish state here, but it will be a different sort, strange and ugly.

    There is time to change course, but not much. What is needed is a new vision of a just society and the political will to implement it. Nor is this merely an internal Israeli affair. Diaspora Jews for whom Israel is a central pillar of their identity must pay heed and speak out. If the pillar collapses, the upper floors will come crashing down.

    The opposition does not exist, and the coalition, with Arik Sharon at its head, claims the right to remain silent. In a nation of chatterboxes, everyone has suddenly fallen dumb, because there's nothing left to say. We live in a thunderously failed reality. Yes, we have revived the Hebrew language, created a marvelous theater and a strong national currency. Our Jewish minds are as sharp as ever. We are traded on the Nasdaq. But is this why we created a state? The Jewish people did not survive for two millennia in order to pioneer new weaponry, computer security programs or anti-missile missiles. We were supposed to be a light unto the nations. In this we have failed.

    It turns out that the 2,000-year struggle for Jewish survival comes down to a state of settlements, run by an amoral clique of corrupt lawbreakers who are deaf both to their citizens and to their enemies. A state lacking justice cannot survive. More and more Israelis are coming to understand this as they ask their children where they expect to live in 25 years. Children who are honest admit, to their parents' shock, that they do not know. The countdown to the end of Israeli society has begun.

    It is very comfortable to be a Zionist in West Bank settlements such as Beit El and Ofra.

    The biblical landscape is charming. From the window you can gaze through the geraniums and bougainvilleas and not see the occupation. Traveling on the fast highway that takes you from Ramot

A Century of Flight

on Jerusalem's northern edge to Gilo on the southern edge, a 12-minute trip that skirts barely a half mile west of the Palestinian roadblocks, it's hard to comprehend the humiliating experience of the despised Arab who must creep for hours along the pocked, blockaded roads assigned to him. One road for the occupier, one road for the occupied.

This cannot work. Even if the Arabs lower their heads and swallow their shame and anger forever, it won't work. A structure built on human callousness will inevitably collapse in on itself. Note this moment well: Zionism's superstructure is already collapsing like a cheap Jerusalem wedding hall. Only madmen continue dancing on the top floor while the pillars below are collapsing. [9]

How can one add to this? One does not find such thoughts in our usual media, certainly not in TV news. The impressive background of the writer and the fact that it was published in a New York Jewish newspaper offer very high credibility. I like to read newspapers but I often find them tame, often (not always) full of managed news by a press corps "ever more courtier-like". What happened to the hawks with millions of dollars spent to investigate Monica and Whitewater? Back in the Reagan days it was only the religious press (including *The Lutheran*) who printed the reality of the Contras and the right wing death squads in Central America. The secular press never did "get it" until it was over. [10] And the Wall Street Journal never did apologize. But now everyone knows the truth about the assassination of Archbishop Romero and much more. Now I had better get back to some chuckles with Molly Ivins.

---

[9] The article was translated by J. J. Goldberg. For the complete essay, go to the CMEP web site: http://www.cmep.org/Alerts/2003sep22.htm. Formed in 1984, Churches for Middle East Peace is a Washington-based ecumenical program at 110 Maryland Ave. NE, #311, Washington, D.C. 20002.

[10] For further information: MENET@LISTSERVE.ELCA.ORG. See also www.holyland-lutherans.org/amman. Also: www.elca.org/middleeast. Also: www.loga.org.

Political Rallies Sharpen the Message

February 2, 2004

A few months ago I walked down the street a few blocks and merged with a crowd estimated at 4000 people to hear Howard Dean attack the Bush administration. It was great fun at long last to hear a Democrat with backbone. Cheers and applause greeted every other line. Dean may not win the primaries but he has certainly tapped a store of unharnessed energy as well as a store of pent-up anger against the Bush administration and the direction in which he is leading the country.

It has been said that the candidates are spoiling for a fight but it is also evident that the Democratic Party urgently needs this fight to sharpen its message. For too long it has meekly withheld criticism under the bumper sticker slogan of "united we stand," while the Bush cabal has changed the country's direction under the mantle of fighting terrorism. The election this fall is not simply about personalities; it is about the direction of the country.

Will the Republican Party have unchecked power in all branches of the government? Although the American voters appear more or less evenly divided, there is no doubt that governmental power does not reflect the balance of public opinion, according to Paul Starr, an editor of The American Prospect. Republican control of the House is obvious and the Senate is nearly so. Appointments to the Supreme Court can be expected within the next term. Will they be clones of Thomas or Scalia? Starr noted that "The Republicans have created so tight a system of financial and political control that it will take little short of a national upheaval to oust them from Congress". He added:

> Objectively the chances of a Democrat winning the presidency are not very high. Massive deficits and extremely low interest rates are giving the economy (and the stock market) an adrenaline rush that should last through the year. Iraq will probably remain stable enough

to be painted a success. The one hope Democrats have is that voters will resist the sheer radicalism of the Bush presidency.

But if a Democrat does win, he will face huge deficits and a Republican Congress unwilling to repeal the Bush tax cuts. Where a Democratic president would immediately matter is in the conduct of war and peace, protection of civil liberties, separation of church and state, environmental regulation, and judicial nominations that would likely affect such key concerns as reproductive freedom and affirmative action. A Democratic president would likely block new moves to privatize Medicare and Social Security and to shift taxes away from the rich. [1]

Because of entrenched power, Starr's opinion is that a Democratic victory this year would be "chiefly defensive: checking the radical agenda that Republicans are pursuing". It is a radical agenda and for that reason I used the word "cabal" in the second paragraph above, well aware of the dictionary definition that it means a "conspiratorial group of planners". According to a book review on *The Great Unraveling: Losing Our Way in the New Century*, the author, a Princeton economist and a columnist, Paul Krugman, is much concerned about the Bush administration's "systematic deception of the public" and "he posits the existence of a revolutionary right-wing conspiracy—a term he does not use lightly". [2] The word "cabal" is not out of place as we become aware of the background activities of Bush's close associates, Karl Rove, Donald Rumsfeld, Paul Wolfowitz, and Richard Cheney.

Sheer Radicalism

Historian and editor Harold Meyerson, has made a case for the radical nature of this administration, stating that Bush seems determined "to extirpate...the basic forms of common security in America," targeting Medicare, which he would privatize, making it available for those who can pay, and Social Security, which he would also privatize. Another target is the United Nations and a large structure of international laws and treaties. Moreover, Myerson states:

---

[1] Paul Starr, "The Republican Lock," *The American Prospect*, Feb. 2004, p. 3.

[2] Richard Cooper, book review of *The Great Unraveling* by Paul Krugman in *Foreign Affairs*, January/February 2004, p. 170. Krugman has credibility teaching in the field of economics but, dismayed by political directions, in the last few years he has been writing columns for *The New York Times*. Note also a book by James C. Moore, entitled: *Bush's Brain: How Karl Rove Made George W. Bush Presidential*

Underpinning these assaults is a decided preference for a more social (and international) Darwinistic order—though in this uniquely Old Testament White House, Darwinism is the love whose name cannot be spoken...

And so, by strategy, inclination and conviction, George W. Bush has been pursuing a reckless, even ridiculous, but always right-wing agenda—shredding a global security structure at a time requiring unprecedented international integration, shredding a domestic safety net at a time when the private sector provides radically less security than it did a generation ago. No American president has ever played quite so fast and loose with the well-being of the American people. [3]

In matters of foreign policy Meyerson claims that this administration appears to be a "coalition of religious and secular millenarians". Christian fundamentalists and right-wing evangelicals are much involved in Republican politics and, for instance, have called the United Nations and other forms of international order the arms of Satan. There is another aspect in that, according to Meyerson, "a growing number of religious Armageddonists...see chaos in the Middle East as a prelude to the coming rapture". This view is tied to various steps to be taken by Israel. [4]

On the other hand, Meyerson states that the neoconservatives provide most of the intellectual direction for this administration and they have a secular dream of the millenium—a new American empire, but not as God's kingdom. Instead, "they see it—better yet—as their own". The neocons consider international structures, such as the United Nations, the European Union, the International Criminal Court, as "obstacles to the emergence of unchallenged American hegemony". Further, he quotes several journalists who have reported that "growing Islamic militance in the Arab world is precisely what the neos want; it justifies the United States in extending the conflict to other nations until the entire region is transformed".

---

[3] Harold Meyerson, "The Most Dangerous President Ever," *The American Prospect*, May 2003, pp. 25-28.

[4] Walter Russell Mead, book reviews, *Foreign Affairs*, Jan./Feb. 2004, 174. In these book reviews Mead wrote that "Conservative evangelicals have been getting most of the publicity lately, but evangelical Christians represent only one facet of Christianity in the United States... Both books are timely reminders of the wealth and diversity of the American religious tradition. Whether looking at liberal or conservative tendencies, it is hard to overestimate the importance of religion in U.S. foreign policy". The books he reviewed were *A People Adrift: The Crisis of the Roman Catholic Church in America* by Peter Steinfels and *The Serenity Prayer: Faith and Politics in Times of Peace and War* by Elisabeth Sifton (the daughter of Reinhold Niebuhr).

Political Rallies Sharpen the Message

Needed: a movement

Particular arguments against the Bush administration can be made under many topics but Robert B. Reich, a former U.S. secretary of labor, states that the Democrats need to mobilize a movement and perhaps a "fierce battle for the White House" may serve "to restore a two-party system of governance and a clear understanding of the choices we face". Reich suggests that Democrats should study what Republicans have learned about winning elections:

> First, it is crucial to build a political movement that will endure after particular electoral contests. Second, in order for a presidency to be effective, it needs a movement that mobilizes Americans behind it. Finally, any political movement derives its durability from the clarity of its convictions. And there's no better way to clarify convictions that to hone them in political combat.
>
> Democrats could have responded [to the right-wing's advances] with bold plans on jobs, schools, health care, and retirement security. They could have delivered a strong message about the responsibility of corporations to help their employees in all these respects, and of wealthy elites not to corrupt politics with money. More recently, the party could have used the threat of terrorism to inspire the same sort of sacrifice and social solidarity as Democrats did in World War II— including higher taxes on the wealthy to pay for what needs doing. In short, they could have turned themselves into a populist movement to take back democracy from increasingly concentrated wealth and power.[5]

Democrats now have a number of champions who have shed their timidity, although they appear to be speaking individually rather than speaking within a movement. Moreover, thanks to the battle for the primaries, the media are beginning to give attention to serious criticism.

Troubling patterns

The former vice president, Al Gore, in a New York City address told the audience about a troubling pattern in the Bush-Cheney administration's approach to almost all issues:

---

[5] Robert B. Reich, "The Dead Center," *New York Times,* Jan. 29, 2004. Reich is a professor of social and economic policy at Brandeis University and he was a founder of *The American Prospect* magazine.

In almost every policy area, the administration's consistent goal has been to eliminate any constraints on their exercise of raw power, whether by law, regulation, alliance or treaty. And in the process, they have in each case caused America to be seen by the other nations of the world as showing disdain for the international community.

They devise their policies with as much secrecy as possible and in close cooperation with the most powerful special interests that have a monetary stake in what happens. In each case, the public interest is not only ignored, but actively undermined. In each case they devote considerable attention to a clever strategy of deception that appears designed to prevent the American people from discerning what it is they are actually doing.

Indeed, they often use Orwellian language to disguise their true purposes. For example, a policy that opens national forests to destructive logging of old-growth trees is labeled Healthy Forest Initiative. A policy that vastly increases the amount of pollution that can be dumped into the air is called the Clear Skies Initiative. [6]

The current drive for power and the deliberate use of deceit are highlighted by an influential author, Kevin Phillips, whose roots are surprisingly Republican. Back in 1969 he wrote *The Emerging Republican Majority*, which, incidentally, was dedicated to Richard Nixon and John Mitchell. According to Michael Oreskes, this book was so powerful because Phillips is not a writer of history but is "an analyst of demographics and documents, voting patterns and capital accumulation". [7] Leaving the Republican Party to become an Independent, Phillips has now written *American Dynasty: Aristocracy, Fortune, and the Politics of Deceit in the House of Bush*. Tracing the family through four generations, he described patterns of secrecy and deception in their accumulation of power and money. Phillips wrote that

> George W. Bush's behavior, far from being entirely his own product, is rooted in the dynasty's four-generation evolution and concomitant pattern of deception, dissimulation and disinformation.

---

[6] Quoted in Bob Herbert, "Masters of Deception," *The New York Times*, Jan. 16, 2004. Herbert added: "The fates dealt Mr. Gore and the United States a weird hand in 2000. He got the most votes but the other guy became president. And the country, its Treasury looted and its most pressing needs deliberately ignored, has been rolling backward ever since".

[7] Michael Oreskes, "Family Lies," a book review of *American Dynasty: Aristocracy, Fortune, and the Politics of Deceit in the House of Bush* by Kevin Phillips, *New York Times Book Review*, Jan. 18, 2004.

Further evidence of secret planning and deception by this administration has been unveiled in the statements of Paul O'Neill, who had resigned as the Treasury secretary. According to one reviewer, O'Neill confirmed much that had been suspected: "Bush is arrogant, incurious and out of touch; Dick Cheney is the power behind the throne; planning for an invasion of Iraq began long before 9/11; and economic policy was designed to benefit the wealthy at everyone else's expense". [8]

Politics and Religion

During the Cold War many of the Christian fundamentalists and right-wing evangelicals appeared to consider ethics as an aspect of individual piety, clearly evident in their condemnation of the social statements of various church bodies and the National Council of Churches. In later decades they dramatically changed their views and right-wing churches became centers of political activism, strangely allied to the secular millenarians in Republican circles and clearly identified with the "movement".

There is no doubt that social involvement has strong support in Scriptures, both Old and New Testaments. The prophet Amos, for example, denounced Israel for reliance on military might, for injustice ("who oppress the poor and crush the needy") and for their meaningless piety. The Christian churches in America all express support for ethical social concepts but, except for the right wing, they are not working within a cohesive movement. Recognizing that public policy in America is often shaped by the private interests of the strong and powerful, it is obvious that ethical concern will be effective only as the expression of a movement.

America's founders established the respected tradition of the separation of church and state, which the Christian right wing is trying to break. One can readily imagine the result of their alliance with the power of government—medieval thoughts in modern dress. Writing on this issue, Gary Wills has written that

> No matter how much Jefferson and Madison tried to pitchfork religion out of official governmental actions, it has kept sneaking back in… Madison said that religion is "not within the cognizance of civil government." He did not even want ministers of religion to list their profession in the government's census, since "the general

---

[8] Jeff Baker, "Inside the Oval Office," *The Oregonian* (n.d.). O'Neill's account appears in the recent publication of *The Price of Loyalty: George W. Bush, the White House, and the Education of Paul O'Neill* by Ron Suskind.

government is proscribed from interfering, in any manner whatever, in matters respecting religion... Madison would be surprised at how much religion gets "cognized" in, say, Karl Rove's Rolodex.[9]

As a concluding thought for this paper, Gary Wills referred to Mark Twain's bitterness as America engaged in one of its preemptive wars—this one in the Philippines near the turn of the century—and quoted a prayer for that time. Thinking of the unnecessary war in Iraq brought about by the Bush cabal, here is Mark Twain's War Prayer (in part), as quoted by Wills:

> O Lord our God, help us to tear their soldiers to bloody shreds with our shells; help us to cover their smiling fields with the pale forms of their patriot dead; help us to drown the thunder of the guns with the shrieks of their wounded, writhing in pain; help us to lay waste their humble homes with a hurricane of fire, ... help us to turn them out roofless with their little children to wander unfriended the wastes of their desolated land... We ask it in the spirit of love, of Him Who is the Source of Love.

---

[9] Gary Wills, "With God On His Side," *New York Times Magazine,* March 30, 2003.

38

New Forms of Christianity

March 29, 2004

New Global Concepts

A current journal of theology suggests that in this new century we will see a new form of Christianity "as distinct as Protestantism or Orthodoxy" along with a blurring of traditional denominational lines. Conversation with a friend prompted me to think of political parallels, in which we can see a blurring of the powers of national sovereignty, a blurring of the distinctions of the executive, legislative and judicial branches, and a dismantling of the structures which support a middle class. It might be argued that the suggested changes in Christianity are not necessarily bad, but the picture of a twenty-first century feudalism in which the manor houses are actually global corporations and the middle class has been reduced to serfdom is not an appealing picture.

A New Christianity?

This is the theme of the current issue of *Dialog, A Journal of Theology* (Spring 2004), in which the starting point is a study by Philip Jenkins, the author of *The Next Christendom* (Oxford, 2002), who forecasts the rise of a Third Church with roots in Africa, Asia and Latin America, a church which in his view is likely to be dominant. Describing the contents of this issue, *Dialog's* editor, Ted Peters, wrote: "What I perceive...is the widespread assumption that the world of tomorrow will be characterized by religious pluralism accompanied by a risk of a "clash of civilizations". [1]

The journal's leading article, entitled "Demographic Futures for Christianity and the World Religions" was written by Todd M. Johnson, on the faculty of Gordon-Conwell Theological Seminary in

---

[1] Ted Peters, "A New Christianity?" (editorial), *Dialog, A Journal of Theology, vol.* 43:1 (Spring 2004), p. 2.

Massachusetts. ² As director of the Center for the Study of Global Christianity and co-author of *World Christian Encyclopedia*, the author is well prepared to present various statistical tables with a forecast of trends in the demographics of world religions.

It is well known that in demographics Christianity has been declining in the North and growing rapidly in the South. Johnson pointed out that in 1900 over 81% of Christians were white but by the year 2000 only 45% were white. He added that "Kinshasa, Buenos Aires, Addis Ababa, and Manila are replacing Rome, Athens, Paris, London and New York as the new centers of Christianity" and that "Churches in the South are more traditional, conservative, and apocalyptic than those in the North". Moreover, he stated that the "rapid growth of conservative Christianity in Muslim contexts in Nigeria, Indonesia, and the Philippines sets up a potential 'clash of civilizations'." Referring to the studies of Philip Jenkins, Danish theologian Viggo Mortensen, has described the future look of Christendom in this way:

> By the year 2050, at least six nations, i.e., Brazil, Mexico, the Philippines, Nigeria, Congo and the US will have more than 100 million Christians. Africa south of Sahara will long have overtaken Europe in the number of Christians. Brazil will have 150 million Catholics and 40 million Protestants. And more than a billion Pentecostals will spread their version of Christianity.
>
> [Moreover] in the southern hemisphere we will see a wave of non-democratic states with theocratic tendencies... If these Christians can manage to avoid fighting between themselves, they will gang up against the common enemy, Islam. 10 out of the 25 largest states will either be Christian or Islamic and at least 10 will be the scenes of bloody conflicts. ³

An example of sharp demographic changes was heard at the general assembly of the Lutheran World Federation, meeting in Winnipeg, Canada, in July 2003. It was noted that the retiring president of the LWF, Bishop Christian Krause, "reported that the membership of his Lutheran Church in Braunschweig, Germany, had decreased from

---

² Todd M. Johnson, "Demographic Futures for Christianity and the World Religions," *Dialog* (Spring 2004), pp. 10-19.

³ Viggo Mortensen, "What Is Happening to Global Christianity?" *Dialog* (Spring 2004), p. 21. Mortensen is on the Theological Faculty at the University of Aarhus, Denmark, and previously served as director for the Department for Theology and Studies in the Lutheran World Federation in Geneva.

700,000 to 420,000 over the past 30 years. During the same time, the MekaneYesu [Lutheran] Church in Ethiopia has increased its membership from 700,000 to 4 million". [4]

Many sociologists have predicted the decline of religion, holding that religion would become irrelevant. Johnson quoted one writer who stated: "From Voltaire to Marx every Enlightenment thinker thought that religion would disappear in the 20th century because religion was fetishism, animistic superstition". Within the span of my own lifetime I can recall instances which reflect a shifting of attitudes. For example, in my youth a medical doctor expressed polite disdain for any view of health which included one's emotions. His materialistic framework certainly had no place for religion and I wonder how he treated ulcers. Another example: back in the 1960s it was stated that one tangential result of the civil rights struggle was the irrefutable evidence that the churches were no longer irrelevant. Moreover, it is obvious that religion is a significant factor in current political equations.

In early readings of Dietrich Bonhoeffer during my student days I had difficulty understanding some of his terms, such as the "post-Christian" age. Other writers have labeled certain periods of time, referring, for example, to a "post-modern" age, in which religion would have no significance in public matters. Briefly Mortensen traced the relation between modernization and secularization from the Reformation and the Enlightenment to modern times with emphases on individualism and the place of reason. The topic of secularization was a key topic of interest following World War II when many thought that "religion was a thing of the past". Mortensen wrote:

> Statistics show this development in a slackening of the institutional discipline. People are not actively involved with the institutional church, but they do not abandon their affiliation. People have not stopped believing... As Christianity was the prevalent religion in Europe, this also meant a de-religionisation or, at least, a dilution of religion to such an extent that it was not always sufficient to satisfy the religious feeling, which was the reason why people looked around to have the empty space filled up. Secularization and the appearance of the new religious movements thus became interrelated. [5]

---

[4] Hans Raun Iversen, "Religion in the 21st Century," *Dialog,* (Spring 2004), p. 32.

[5] Mortensen, "What Is Happening to Global Christianity?" p. 23.

What do these trends indicate for the future? Johnson claimed that secularization "comes up short," quoting *Dialog* editor Ted Peters that "future consciousness itself is an intensely religious phenomenon". Several writers have drawn attention to ecumenical trends. The chasms between Catholicism, Orthodoxy and Protestantism appear to be diminishing. [6] Regarding ecumenical directions, Danish theologian Niels H. Gregersen expressed the hope that the Lutheran World Federation would "take the first steps" not only toward the Orthodox and the Roman Catholic Churches, but also towards the Pentecostal Movement. [7] Moreover, there will be interaction between Christianity and Islam, Hinduism and Buddhism. Johnson also anticipates "an increasingly complex interaction between religion and politics...in the global South". As an indication of these trends, I just received a catalog from the Graduate Theological Union (GTU) in Berkeley in which one course of study was entitled "Martin Luther and Buddhism," which would "examine the theology of Martin Luther in light of Buddhist-Christian dialog," a course which was also offered last year.

Mortensen has written of two trends in Christianity. One will lead to diversity and variety in which the church will respond to the different segments of fragmented societies. The second trend will lead to uniformity, which he calls the "McDonaldization of the church," the title of a book by John Drane, referring to "efficiency, calculability, predictability and control". Unfortunately Mortensen did not offer much explanation on this point. However, Mortensen did present a challenge:

> If we do not think fundamentalism, relativism or syncretism is the right answer for the future of global Christianity, we must work for alternatives now. In this endeavor dialogue must be central—dialogue between cultures and dialogue between religions. [8]

He added that Lutherans should share with other Christians an agenda which includes a channeling of love for the neighbor through the institutions of society.

---

[6] Johnson, op. cit., p. 12. See references to Karl Rahner and Hans Küng.

[7] Niels Henrik Gregersen, "New Ecumenical Tasks and Challenges," *Dialog* (Spring 2004), p. 6.

[8] Mortensen, op. cit., p 26.

A 21st-Century Feudalism

As denominational lines have blurred among churches and their place in society is changing, so also in politics the lines of traditional views are blurred and new realities present new challenges. For example, the words "liberal" and "conservative" have been so abused in their use as epithets that their true meanings have been lost. Associated with liberation or freedom, "liberal" describes policies which favor civil liberties and the power of government to further social progress. It might be argued that liberal Democrats have restricted freedom with the growth of government, although the point is debatable. On the other hand one can ask what the Republicans are trying to conserve in their role as "conservatives". Conservatives such as Nelson Rockefeller and Harold Stassen, let alone Teddy Roosevelt are not to be seen in Republican leadership today.

In the March issue of *The American Prospect* there is a 19-page supplement entitled "Liberals and Values". [9] One of the contributors, Matthew Yglesias wrote that at times Democrats have lost votes on particular stands on social issues, although they usually win approval in time. He listed the following examples:

- The civil-rights advances of the mid-1960s were, in their way, a tactical debacle for Democrats, pushing the formerly solid South firmly into the GOP column. But Richard Nixon's "Southern strategy" provoked no move toward resegregation, and such an initiative today is literally unthinkable.
- Similarly, no one is trying to put women back in the kitchen, and public opinion remains firmly in favor of a basic right to reproductive freedom. (...Even George W. Bush has shied away from the rhetorical support Ronald Reagan offered for a total ban.)
- School prayer, eliminated by a liberal U.S. Supreme Court in 1962, likewise seems to have vanished from the discourse for the time being, despite the best of conservative efforts.
- Even on gay rights, liberals keep winning. The Massachusetts marriage ruling came in the wake of the Supreme Court's reversal of anti-sodomy laws, Vermont's institution of a civil-unions scheme, and the Romer V. Evans decision striking down an anti-gay amendment in the Colorado constitution. [10]

Regarding shifts of policy and taxation, Yglesias added the following:

---

[9] *The American Prospect*, March 2004, pp. 34-53.

[10] Matthew Yglesias, "Forward March," *The American Prospect*, March 2004, p. 52.

> Sometime in the Reagan years Democrats essentially stopped making the case for increased public investment and the taxes that go with it, and shifted the conversation to how much tax cutting a deficit-racked nation could afford. Twenty years later, the tax code has only grown more regressive and the deficit is huge... But as they've learned with the Bush tax cuts, a tactical retreat can quickly become a rout. Republicans today face the same problem on cultural matters... [For example, there was] pressure from fellow conservatives to disavow Trent Lott's segregationism, and there's little doubt that today's proponents of a constitutional amendment banning gay marriage will look just as prehistoric a generation from now.

The religious right wing has considerable political clout; nevertheless, it is clear that there are many moderates who consider themselves conservatives but reject a fundamentalist morality.

After a long wait I finally received my library copy of the recent book by Kevin Phillips, *American Dynasty: Aristocracy, Fortune, and the Politics of Deceit in the House of Bush*. Formerly a Republican and a White House strategist, he is the influential author of nine books. Noting in the preface that he came of political age during the Nixon years, his own "distaste since the 1960s for what George H. W. Bush seemed to represent—a career built on support from a vague 'elite' rather than merit or democratic selection—had a Republican genesis," which was evident in his 1990 book, *The Politics of Rich and Poor*. In *American Dynasty* he draws attention to the change of direction with the Bush Republicans, noting the growing trends of favoritism to the top 1 percent and "crony capitalism a la Enron" (with whom the Bush dealings go back to 1986) and a presidency which has been temporary for one or two terms but now appears to be entrenched in a permanent circle of the powerful.

Another book of note is *The Working Poor: Invisible in America* by David K. Shipler. Ron Suskind, in a book review, wrote that Shipler tried to "harness the outrage" by suggesting positive programs, such as job training, early childhood care and remedial education, noting that a Marshall Plan might be needed "considering that 14 percent of American adults can't find an intersection on a map, total a deposit slip or determine the correct dose of a medication". [11] Suskind's statement that this is a "seminal" book is reflected in this quotation:

> Then, the questions tend to be about the "hows"—how we, as a country, might now act. Readers, by the last page, can scarcely avoid

---

[11] Ron Suskind, book review on *The Working Poor: Invisible in America* by David K. Shipler, *New York Times Book Review*, F, 2004, p. 7.

New Forms of Christianity

that question, or the larger algorithm that Shipler offers: "To appraise a society, examine its ability to be self-correcting. When grievous wrongs are done or endemic suffering exposed, when injustice is discovered or opportunity denied, watch the institutions of government and business and charity. Their response is an index of a nation's health and of a people's strength.

It is becoming apparent that journalists and the "loyal opposition" are waking up to their duties to hold those in power accountable and that the American people are recognizing that patriotism does not negate critical judgment, as evident with current best sellers. The great interest in Richard Clarke and his book, *Against all Enemies*, prompted me to request a copy at the library. Anticipating a reservation list, I learned that the library had 19 copies but, surprisingly, there were 324 requests ahead of me. I have not yet inquired at Powell's Books but I have heard that book stores across the country are sold out and there have already been several printings of the book. This is good news for many of us. Until the recent criticisms raised by such credible authors as Richard Clarke and Paul O'Neal there has been no critical accounting of this administration. For a couple years under the bumper sticker of United We Stand this administration has had a free ride with the media. Moreover, there has been no concerted program of harassment, as with Whitewater and Monica. Instead of spending $40 million or $70 million for investigation by an "independent" counsel, Democratic leaders have been cooperative with the Republican leadership. It is now obvious that the king is not above judgment. [12]

---

[12] Overheard in a church coffee hour: "Blessed are they who wrap themselves in the flag of nine/eleven and stonewall the investigating commission. May hypocrisy be theirs".

39

Piety and Fascism

May 18, 2004

G. B. Shaw's "Man and Superman"
Having just come across some notes I wrote a year or so ago after seeing George Bernard Shaw's play, "Man and Superman," I asked Sandra to refresh my memory. In a moment she gave me the full text and during the next hour's reading the scenes of the play came back to mind. Shaw was a freethinker who, certainly against the times, supported women's rights and advocated equality of income. Notes from the program stated that in 1884 Shaw

> became a charter member of the Fabian Society along with other British intellectuals... Fabians believed that capitalism had created an unjust and inefficient society... Character—national, individual, moral—was a Victorian preoccupation, but Fabians took it further believing that its development in the individual was a form of liberation from oppression. [Moreover] Fabians believed in the gradual, peaceful change of society through democratic methods such as education, lecturing, and discussions. [1]

These are the very themes which are behind the headlines of today's news.

Piety and Fascism
Matthew Fox, formerly a Dominican priest, wrote an article in which he linked Mel Gibson's controversial film The Passion with a fascist culture, noting that the "piety of fascism is inevitably a piety of pain and suffering". [2] With its emphasis on blood and gore, Fox claimed that the film is a "monument to sadomasochism...making Jesus a victim rather than a martyr while removing Jesus' passion for

---

[1] Cynthia Kirk, "Politics, His Passion," Program for George Bernard Shaw, "Man and Superman," Portland Center for the Performing Arts.

[2] Matthew Fox, "Mel Gibson's Passion and Fascism's Piety of Pain," an article which came my way from a friend who obtained it from the Internet.

justice" and having nothing at all to say about God's grace. Explaining his terms, Fox wrote:

> Our culture is deeply engaged in sadomasochism—understood here as the haves lording over the have-nots. How so? Let's take contemporary capitalism and the world distribution of wealth and power as an example: In the 1960s, the overall income of the richest 20 percent of the world's population was thirty times that of the poorest 20 percent. Today, it is 224 times larger… It would take no more than 5 percent of the overall annual sales of arms in the world to feed all the starving children, to protect them from dying of preventable diseases, and to make basic education accessible to all. Yet Gibson's Jesus shows none of the passion for justice that served as a corrective to the sadomasochistic tendencies of his own culture and times… [3]

Matthew Fox was critical of tendencies toward authoritarian practices in Christianity. In Roman Catholicism he mentioned the Second Vatican Council as "an attempt to throw off fascism in the Catholic Church" and he pointed to the current pope's efforts to dilute the effect of liberation theology. Regarding the right wing of Protestantism, he wrote:

> It is no wonder, then, that [Gibson's] film is being seen by so many Christian groups whose piety is built more on fear than it is on love and hope, more on sin than on blessing, more on victimization than on liberation. No wonder Gibson leaves out so much of the message of Jesus: It is not compatible with fascism which is about control and not justice, about power-over, not power-with (compassion).

In this context the extreme right wing of Protestantism comes to mind. As an example of the drive for power, Christian Zionists are committed and focused in their ideology and have considerable influence at the White House. They hold that the formation of the political state of Israel in 1948 was God's intention that the "children of Israel be gathered 'to Jerusalem'" in anticipation of the Second Coming. Moreover, according to Michael Prior, a scholar in Holy Land Studies, Christian Zionists believe they can aid God's plan in moving up the time table for the Armageddon Massacre—a far cry from Jesus'

---

[3] Gibson's personal identification with a pre-Vatican II authoritarian Roman Catholicism has been reported. Fox stated that Gibson is "allegedly a member of Opus Dei, a secretive Catholic sect," and noted that Opus Dei's founder, the Spanish priest Escriva, was rushed into canonization two years ago.

exhortations during his first Coming to feed the hungry, give sight to the blind, and clothe the naked. [4]

> Fascism is defined by Matthew Fox as
> An authoritarianism that swamps all else—conscience, community, human rights, justice—and that in the process legitimizes violence. Fascism is a philosophy of disempowerment based on fear, power over (sadism), power under (masochism), victimhood, and scapegoating. Fascism seems to need religion and even religious piety to wrap around itself... It's God is the God of Authoritarianism.

Is there any doubt that many in Protestantism's right wing favor and actively promote an authoritarian pattern in church and family life and extend this pattern in their goals for government? Many evangelicals (common usage of this word) and fundamentalists actively promote a linkage of the power of the state with their religious goals. I recall that in the early years of my ministry the Protestant right wing churches (labels are difficult) kept themselves aloof from social-political issues. They were also unhappy with the translation of the Revised Standard Version (RSV) of the Bible because it was sponsored by the National Council of Churches, which was issuing some controversial social statements, although at the time they applauded a loose, street-level version. A bumper sticker at the time stated clearly "The Bible said it. I believe it. That settles it." Roman Catholicism was also clearly authoritarian, especially prior to the Second Vatican Council.

Is it not a truism that the ends meet? Consider the political extremes of the left and the right. They both meet in authoritarianism and with little encouragement they reform in totalitarianism. The leftist extreme was Stalinist communism and the rightist extreme was Hitler's fascism. Numerous factors are evident in these ends, such as strong symbols of nationalism (wave the flag), disdain for human rights—trumped by security needs, enemies as scapegoats, supremacy of the military, obsession with national security, intertwining of religion and government, and protection of corporate power. [5]

---

[4] Michael Prior, C.M., "The Holy Land and the Scandalous Performance of the Churches," *Cornerstone* Issue 30 (Winter 2003), a publication of Sabeel, an Ecumenical Liberation Theology Center, whose leadership is related to the Anglican Church. Dr. Prior is a Senior Research Fellow at St. Mary's College, University of Surrey, U.K.

[5] These factors are among the fourteen characteristics of fascism proposed by Dr. Lawrence Britt, quoted by Matthew Fox as noted above.

Piety and Fascism

Can any thoughtful person not see parallels in the direction in which this country is being prodded? Anthony Lewis, a respected journalist, recently wrote:

> Suppression of civil liberty in the name of national security is an old story... We are in another bad time for civil liberties now. Under the mantle of his War on Terror, President Bush has imprisoned American citizens without trial, detained thousands of aliens in this country, and persuaded Congress to let government intrude more deeply into our private lives. In a significant respect, the danger to liberty is more serious than in past episodes. [6]

Reviewing Michael Ignatieff's book, *The Lesser Evil: Political Ethics in an Age of Terror*, Lewis noted that the author draws attention to the need for "awareness and sensitivity" in balancing the interests of security and liberty but claims that there is a "bleak absence" of these qualities in Bush and his people. The author criticized American courts for their habit of "deferring too readily to executive claims of military necessity, as in the Japanese internment decision". For example, the Bush administration has held two American citizens without trial for more than twenty-two months, arguing that they are "enemy combatants"—an elusive category. Lewis stated that this administration is "vigorously—I would say obsessively—maintaining that they should have no meaningful chance to contest that designation in court...and have no right to consult a lawyer". Various other examples are given, such as the case of the American citizen Jose Padilla, now before the Supreme Court as well as Attorney General Ashcroft's harsh treatment and detention of aliens.

Questions should also be raised regarding the "unlawful combatants" held at Guantánamo. Could this be an American version of France's nineteenth-century Devil's Island? There is little doubt that this Bush administration is blurring the constitutional distinctions of the three branches of government, executive, legislative and judicial. If citizens can be arrested and detained indefinitely without any recourse to counsel or courts simply at the whim of the president, is it not time for the successors of Alexander Hamilton and James Madison to write another series of essays, a defense against the abuses of King George (the II or IV)?

---

[6] Anthony Lewis, "Bush and the Lesser Evil," *The New York Review*, May 27, 2004. This title was a review of: Michael Ignatieff, *The Lesser Evil: Political Ethics in an Age of Terror* (Princeton) and an article by the same author, Michael Ignatieff, "The Year of Living Dangerously: A Liberal Supporter of the War Looks Back" (*New York Times Magazine*).

Vision, Purpose or Simply Extrication

> In Washington an age of moral and philosophical sterility is deeply entrenched [and] the decline dates from the end of the cold war, which suddenly and shockingly left Washington without any purpose that could be called visionary or even faintly noble. [7]

There have been hints of a grand vision for the Middle East in the rhetoric of the neocons, such as reshaping the Middle East with models of democracy, beginning with Iraq, which would welcome with open arms a liberation brought by American soldiers. The great vision, however, has been downgraded to purposes, which one after another have been found without substance. Is the purpose actually imperialism or colonialism or the quest for oil? The one cause which is stoutly maintained by the Bush people is that we are in a war against terror. Although Iraq was not linked to Osama bin Laden, Bush owes his spurt of popularity to a strong defense against terroristic attacks (United We Stand) and the war continues to be his political raison d'etre.

If there is no credible vision or purpose, the alternative appears to be extrication. Peter W. Galbraith has offered a thoughtful article, "How to Get Out of Iraq," in which he quoted a European diplomat who told him about "china shop rules in Iraq: you break it, you pay for it." [8] Seriously, he concluded with these words:

> I believe United States policy is most successful when it follows international law and works within the United Nations, according to the provisions of the Charter. This is not just a matter of upholding the ideals of the UN; it is also practical. As our war in Iraq demonstrates, we cannot afford any other course.

The "fundamental problem of Iraq is an absence of Iraqis," according to Galbraith, who referred to the three principal groupings of people in the current boundaries. In the north the Kurds have no desire to be part of Iraq. Their eighty years of association with Iraq have been painful. However, the independence they long for would be firmly opposed by Turkey and Syria, which both have significant Kurdish populations. In the south the majority Shiites, who have long been

---

[7] Russell Baker, "In Bush's Washington," *The New York Review,* May 13, 2004, p. 24.

[8] Peter W. Galbraith, "How to Get Out of Iraq," *The New York Review,* May 13, 2004, pp. 42-46.

repressed, express their identity through religion and long to wield power. In the center are the Sunnis, without organization and leader but include many of Iraq's professionals, who had served with the Baath Party.

Galbraith stated his opinion that "Iraq is not salvageable as a unitary state," although U.S. strategy is to establish a strong central government. In his view federalism would make Kurdistan in the north and the Shiites in the south governable because there are responsible parties in those areas. Lessening restrictions against those who had been associated with the Baathists mig ht provide organizational leaders for the mixed central area. Galbraith's conclusion stated that "Iraq demonstrates all too clearly the folly of the preventive war doctrine and unilateralism".

An Imam Reading Martin Luther?

Mansour al-Nogaidan, once a devoted ultra-Islamist as a "hard-core imam," has turned to liberal views, defying the narrow views of Wahhabism in Saudi Arabia and reading Nietzsche, Habermas and books of history. From an interview by Elizabeth Rubin:

> Most dear to him these days, however, is a biography of Martin Luther, which surprised and inspired him. For Martin Luther was not what Mansour had expected—a soft messenger of God. Instead, Mansour discovered that Luther was tough with his enemies… Mansour had just spent five days in prison for his recent anti-Wahhabist writing, and he told me that he often turns for strength to a story about Luther and Erasmus… "When Erasmus told Luther to calm down and be polite," Mansour said, "Luther told Eramus: this is war". [9]

---

[9] Elizabeth Rubin, "The Jihadi Who Kept Asking Why," *New York Times Magazine, March 7, 2004, p. 34 ff.*

Church and State: Dialogue or Clash

August 2, 2004

The terrorist attacks, followed by the war in Afghanistan, turned to new directions in which the threat of terror has allowed an unrelated war and the curtailment of established principles and ideals. Not only have individual rights been diminished (library choices profiled) but the three branches of government are threatened with imbalance. In particular, the lines between church and state have become blurred in the United States. As Muslims are being labeled and criticized for the mixing of their religious zeal with politics there is urgent need to examine the sharply different cultural perspectives which are given emotional intensity by religious loyalties both in Islam and in Christianity.

How do we in the United States understand ourselves as a nation vis-à-vis widespread criticism in the world? Are battle lines now forming for another Cold War? This has been suggested by the noted historian Samuel Huntington's popular title *The Clash of Civilizations and the Remaking of World Order*. On the other hand, will dialogue and discussion be encouraged?

At the time of the terrorist attacks Joshua Messner, guest editor of *The Cresset*, wrote that universities were unprepared to face the need to learn "more about the turbulent politics of the Middle East and the enigmatic culture surrounding Islam," noting that Arabic language studies reported 60% increases. [1] Universities across the land were pressed to meet the demand for studies. In this readiness for dialogue Messner edited a special edition of The Cresset, dealing with an inter-faith dialogue. "Honest interfaith dialogue," he wrote, "must remember its roots in the Middle East," where the Muslim's faith permeates every aspect of the believer's life, and where a Christian, for example in Palestine, is associated with Western culture, although speech in daily life and worship is in Arabic.

---

[1] Joshua D. Messner, "In luce tua," *The Cresset* LXV: 2 & 3 (Christmas/Epiphany 2001-2002, p. 3. *The Cresset* is published by Valparaiso University.

Over the centuries Christians have had numerous views of how they should regard other religions. On this subject Gerald R. McDermott, who teaches religion at Roanoke College, has written a review essay based on a book by S. Mark Heim, *The Depth of the Riches*.[2] Heim traced the church's general view in the first millennium as it faced great diversity, that there is not salvation outside the church, although there were many modifications of this view. Among others, Pope Gregory VII (d. 1085) "conceded that Muslims who obey the Qur'an might find salvation in the bosom of Abraham, and St. Francis...referred to Muslim 'brothers'." Aquinas later introduced the thought of "implicit faith" and the "baptism of desire".

With the distinctions of pluralism, inclusivism and exclusivism, McDermott was pleased that discussion has been reopened, stating that it gives "Christians the permission to think of other religionists as having truth, perhaps even some they do not share, and finding some good end..." For Christians to engage in dialogue with Muslims is a challenge which should be faced not with bluster but with humility. Speaking of this challenge, Charles Amjad-Ali, a professor at Luther Seminary, listed some necessary understandings in terms and perspectives.[3] One problem is the application of the term "fundamentalism". In the United States its use began in the early 20th century, when it was used in pride by those who ascribed to a set of fundamental beliefs. The term later acquired a negative meanings as it provoked controversy and faced academic and scientific criticism.

The common use of the term "Islamic fundamentalism" carries some risk as an inaccurate label, according to Professor Amjad-Ali. Although it is an umbrella term which can be applied to extremist groups in a number of countries, it cannot be applied universally to Islam. Obviously there are extremists and violent activists in many religions. He also noted the tendency to think of Muslims as Arabs, whereas he stated that only seven percent of Muslims come from the Arabic speaking world.

Regarding the linkage of politics and religion, he asked why this linkage should be strange for Muslims, who believe that religion should be "an integral and even central part of civic life". In opposing

---

[2] Gerald R. McDermott, "True Pluralism," a review essay on *The Depth of the Riches: A Trinitarian Theology of Religious Ends* (Eerdmans, 2001), *The Cresset* (Christmas/Epiphany 2001-2002), pp. 28-32.

[3] Charles Amjad-Ali "How Did We Get Here?" *The Cresset*, op.cit., pp. 9-13.

such a linkage Western Christianity has a legacy to overcome because of it identification with colonialism and economic power. Professor Ajjad-Ali stated:

> The close association of Christian mission with Western imperial power over the last 500 years, especially since the emblematic date of 1844 (the year of the Berlin conference which apportioned Africa) and the largely uncritical approach to colonial expansion by Western churches and missionry structures, has left us very vulnerable to the critique of collusion with Western imperialism.

Moreover, with a probing question regarding the ties of religion and politics, he asked "why it took 1800 years for Christianity to ally itself with a democratic process?" There are those who see the formation of battle lines as the West faces a "new communism" in Islam. On the other hand, according to Amjad-Ali, there are those who argue that "democracy and Islam are not alien to each other". He argued for moderation and a foreign policy capable of nuance. For example, the United States considers Saudi Arabia an ally but his country is the most conservative in the Middle East and it is commonly known that women are not permitted to drive cars and non-Muslims are not permitted to pray, whereas "Iran, by contrast, has at least a dozen women members in its cabinet and has had more elections than any other Middle Eastern country, yet it is not one of our allies". Furthermore [written in 2001],

> Only in two instances has U.S. policy adopted as hard a line toward military authoritarian government as toward radical political Islamists. The two were not fundamentalist Muslim regimes: Qaddafi and Saddam Hussein, both bombed by the U.S. In each of these exceptions, the tag of fundamentalists is absent, but the U.S. turned on them when they turned publicly against the U.S.

Churches for Middle Eat Peace (CMEP) is a "coalition of the public policy offices of national churches and agencies—Orthodox, Catholic and Protestant" which seeks to have a continuing dialogue with Congress and the Administration. [4] These are mainstream religious bodies, which among the Protestant churches includes the Episcopal, Presbyterian, Lutheran and Methodist, but unfortunately their representatives have been unable to meet with President Bush.

---

[4] See www.cmep.org. Additional information is available from www.elca.org/middleeast.

Church and State: Dialogue or Clash

The reluctance of the Bush administration to deal with these churches is not alone because of policies regarding the Middle East but probably also because of differing views on matters of church and state.

In the United States there has been an effective separation of church and state, insisted on by those who drafted the Constitution because they were well aware that the power of either the church or the state had been abused. It is not secret that there are those who want to break down that wall and the current administration is eager for their support. Although the CMEP leaders could not meet with the president, the Rev. Jerry Falwell could, as he reported:

> I told the president last week in the Oval Office, I said, "Sir, there are 80 million of us evangelicals in this country and we've come to look upon you not only as our president, but as a man of God." He said, "Jerry, I'll do my best. You put great pressure on me; I'll do my best not to disappoint you." [5]

But what do others on the right wing say? The Rev. James Dobson stated:

> The liberal elite and the federal court judges and some members of the media are determined to remove every evidence of faith in God from this entire culture. They are determined to control more and more of our private lives.

This is a strange statement vis-à-vis the right wing's open desire to use the power of government to enforce their views. Could it be that the right wing might solve the major problems of the world with simplistic solutions, as Judie Brown, president of the American Life League, has stated?

> As Congress debates the $87 billion Iraq funding bill, we are urging President Bush to ensure that not one dime will go to the pro-death vultures who seek to impose the Western immorality of abortion and contraception [sic] on the recently liberated Iraqi people.

---

[5] "What Can We Expect from the Religious Right in 2004?" People for the American Way (no date). Following quotations are from this source. Additional information is available from *Church and State*, a magazine published by Americans United for Separation of Church and State. See www.au.org. Jerry Falwell has stated: "I hope to see the day when, as in the early days of our country, we won't have any public schools" (*Church and State*, Sept. 2003, p. 12).

However, a most illuminating point is made by America's top lawyer, Attorney General Ashcroft:

> Unique among the nations, America recognized the source of our character as being godly and eternal, not being civic and temporal. And because we have understood that our source is eternal, American has been different. We have no king but Jesus.

In the United States people have been critical of Muslims who have been seen as overly zealous in their religious and cultural loyalties to government. However, such ties are also clearly evident in America and Europe. For example, recent studies show that religion is linked to economic development, according to two Harvard scholars, Robet J. Barro and Rachel M. McCleary, who wrote in the *American Sociological Review*: our central perspective is that religion affects economic outcomes mainly by fostering religious beliefs that influence individual traits such as honesty, work ethic, thrift and openness to strangers." [6] The report pointed out:

> Since the German sociologist Max Weber wrote about the Protestant work ethic and the spirit of capitalism, social scientists, have argued that culture—including religious habits—is part of the complex mix that determines a country's economic health.

The theory that secularization encourages industrialization and wealth is rejected. For example, over the last 30 years countries such as Malaysia, Singapore and South Korea, "have experienced rapid economic growth and the spread of Christianity".

Another evidence of this link is a recent book by Samuel Huntingdon, author of *The Clash of Civilizations*, cited above. In this new work, *Who Are We? The Challenges to America's National Identity*, he said that Americans must "recommit themselves to Anglo-Protestant culture and values…that have been the source of their unity, power, prosperity, and morality as a force for good in the world". [7] In a review of the book, Lawrence Fuchs stated that Huntington worries that Mexican immigrants will "reconquer the territory that the United

---

[6] Felicia R. Lee, "Faith Can Enrich More Than The Soul," *The New York Times*, Jan. 31, 2004.

[7] Lawrence H. Fuchs, "Mr. Huntington;s Nightmare," a review of *Who Are We? The Challenges to America's National Identity* (Simon and Schuster), *The American Prospect*, August 2004, pp. 70-71.

States took from Mexico in the 19th century," as in a "Mexican-American 'Quebecois' movement," although such views have been refuted by two difference and well respected federal commissions, led by Theodore Hesburgh and Barbara Jordan. Moreover, Fuchs claimed that the growth of evangelical Protestantism in Latin America is not a factor as Mexican Americans become integrated in American politics.

In contrast to Huntington and sociological research, a more emotional evidence of the linking of religion and politics is a statement by James Dobson, founder of Focus on the Family, in clear efforts to support a Republican platform which will enforce right wing views:

> We see this time as the climax of the civil war of values that's been raging for 35 years. This is Gettysburg. This is the D-Day, the Stalingrad. We must oppose those who have done so much create the mess that we're in. [8]

Values, however, are not limited to those shouted by the right wing. The war on terror will not be won by resolving Iraq (which was not threatening the U.S.) or by capturing or killing Osama bin Laden. As noted by August Wilson, in our global community, the majority of our fellow human beings are "at the bottom of a social system that leaves them chained to a cycle of poverty and oppression". [9] Colonial "rebels" in 1776 had less about which to rebel than many people in the world today who would be eager for a war on injustice and poverty and economic powers. Wilson added that the Constitution was fused with sanctity [and] George Washington called it 'a sacred obligatory upon all'." Moreover, he insisted that the constitutional separation of church and state must be preserved in the face of vivid examples of the dangers to freedom of choice, and the tyranny that occurs when the state becomes fettered with the demands and obligations of religious beliefs and practice".

Regarding issues of church and state during the 1950s, Lutheran leader Franklin Clark Fry made use of the felicitous phrasing "institutional separation but functional interaction". [10]

---

[8] Quoted in Ralph G. Neas in a report by People for the American Way, July 16, 2004.

[9] August Wilson, "To secure the blessings of liberty," *The Seattle Times*, July 11, 2004

[10] Franklin Clark Fry was president (presiding bishop) in turn of the United Lutheran Church in America and the Lutheran Church in America, as well as the Lutheran World Federation. *Time* magazine called him "Mr. Protestant" and pictured him on the cover.

ISBN 1-41204280-1